Keeping It in the Family

Keeping It in the Family
Successful Succession of the Family Business

James W. Lea, Ph.D.

John Wiley & Sons, Inc.
New York • Chichester • Brisbane • Toronto • Singapore

Copyright © 1991 by James W. Lea

Published by John Wiley & Sons, Inc.

Library of Congress Cataloging in Publication Data
Lea, James (James W.)
    Keeping it in the family : successful succession of the family
  business / James Lea.
      p.   cm.
    Includes bibliographical references.
    ISBN 0-471-53913-9
    1. Family-owner business enterprises—Succession.   I. Title.
  HD62.25.L43   1991
    658.1'6—dc20   90-26862

Printed in the United States of America

10 9 8 7 6 5 4 3 2 1

For Diane, who believes in me.

▌Acknowledgments

A great many people have helped give this book shape and direction. The most help has come from Dick Levin, my mentor in subjects ranging from running companies to buying boats and my close friend. Dick inspired my commitment to family business, as he has inspired thousands of other colleagues and students, and gave me invaluable critiques on parts of this book. Ethen Ellenberg, my literary agent, helped with good ideas and tireless efforts. Steve Ross and Linda Indig at John Wiley & Sons helped with their encouragement and by insisting that their readers deserve the best possible book on succession. Laura Van Toll and Kim Karcher at Impressions, Inc., helped make the manuscript more readable and informative.

A special acknowledgment goes to the thousands of families whose efforts to sustain their businesses through the generations make up this book's heart and substance. They have talked and listened to me, shared their concerns and successes, and fired my enthusiasm. To those men and women, most of all, go my gratitude and great respect.

Preface

"Solving problems is the work of a good mind.

Identifying problems is the work of a higher intellect.

Anticipating problems is the work of all the mental faculties, enhanced by an appreciation of the propensity of human beings for shooting themselves in the foot."

This book has been written with the hope of putting down on paper a few answers to some of the questions that I'm asked about handing over family businesses to the next generation of owners and managers. Business owners stop me in the hall following one of my seminars and tell me things like this: "I've worked for 30 years to build my company, expecting that my children would someday take it over and make careers out of it. Now I'm ready to retire and it seems like they aren't interested. What am I gonna do?"

Business owners' family members ask hallway questions, too: "I really would like to go into my parents' business. But I can't get them to sit down and make some kind of a plan. I've got better things to do with my life than waiting around to see who inherits the company. Is there any way this can be resolved?"

Behind the frustration of such questions are the human factors that influence—in some cases control—the success or failure of family business succession. As in all transfers of business ownership, accounting issues like the valuation of assets, compensation and incentives, and retirement plans play a role in succession. But when an ownership transfer is carried out within a family, accounting issues are often overridden by interpersonal issues, and even the simplest handover of the smallest business becomes a complex, emotionally loaded proposition.

Senior business owners may want their kids to take over their companies, but at the same time they just can't face giving the companies up. Sons and daughters of owners may want to come into their families' businesses, but they don't understand how the businesses work or how to run them successfully. The relationships and traditions that bind a family together can tear it apart when it comes time to pass along the family business—or they can be the basis of a dynamic, durable and profitable family heritage of business ownership and management. The outcomes of succession are often determined by how well the family deals with its own special mix of personalities, priorities and choices.

This book begins with a look at families in business, how they got in business and the chances of their continuing in business for more than one generation. It describes the analytical thinking that senior owners and prospective successors should do about the current characteristics and future needs of both the business and the family, factors at the very heart of successful succession.

Mechanisms for generating and confirming family members' interest in and readiness for succession are discussed in terms of marketing principles. The book describes how to organize a businesslike succession plan and how to make the tough decisions that are inevitable during the ownership and management transition. Finally, it offers some answers to the questions of why, how and when a senior business owner should let go of control and finally pass responsibility and authority to the next generation.

A self-assessment, planning organizer or checklist appears at the end of each chapter to help systematize the planning and management of succession. The Appendix cites additional sources and resources that may also be of help but whose effective application to any specific succession situation can't be guaranteed.

Throughout, this book emphasizes the human factors in family business succession, the stresses they can create and the ways they can be handled. Such fine family virtues as love, respect and shared values can sometimes make business dealings among family members pretty thorny. But those same virtues can also make working together to sustain the family-owned business a rich and rewarding enterprise.

When my grandmother reached her one hundredth birthday, she observed to the assembled family that if she'd known she was going to live so long she'd have taken better care of herself. This book is about how to make sure a solid, satisfying family business lives a long time and how to take care of it—and the family that owns it—in the process.

James W. Lea, Ph.D.

Contents

Checklists   xiii

Introduction   1

1. **A Family Affair**   5
   What Is a Family Business? ▪ Management Dream of Nightmare ▪ Which Businesses Survive Succession . . .? ▪ And Which Ones Don't? ▪Beyond the Second Generation ▪ Will the Family and the Business Mix? ▪ Self Assessment: Is Your Business Ready for Succession?

2. **Analyzing the Factors and Estimating the Odds**   19
   Before Analysis ▪ Analyzing the Business ▪ Analyzing the Family ▪ Analyzing the Owner ▪ The Big Question ▪ Pre-Planning Analysis Checklist

3. **Marketing the Business to the Family**   53
   Why Market the Business to the Family? ▪ The Family Business Marketing Strategy ▪ Marketing Tools and Approaches ▪ The Payoffs of a Successful Marketing Strategy ▪ Family Business Marketing Strategy Checklist

4. **Making the Succession Plan**   83
   Planning Early and Planning Well ▪ Keeping A Clear Head ▪ Who Should Be Involved in Succession Planning? ▪ Choosing and Using Outside Help ▪ The Well-Turned Succession Plan ▪ The Succession Planning Organizer

5. **Being Businesslike**   107
   Succession Management Touchstones ▪ Somebody has to Be the Boss ▪ Planning Fair Financial Incentives and Provisions ▪ Making Rules and Setting Conditions ▪ An Orderly Transfer ▪ Succession Decisions Checklist

6. **Managing the Transition**   133
   Preparing the Next Generation ▪ Delegating Responsibility ▪ Monitoring the Transition Process ▪ Playing By the Rules ▪ When the Transition Plan Isn't Working ▪ The Transition Management Checklist

7. **Letting Go: When, How, and How Much**   159
   Why Letting Go Is Important ▪ Coming Down Easy ▪ Maintaining the Monitoring ▪ How Much Control to Retain—and How ▪ The Last Hurrah ▪ The Letting Go Checklist

8.   **Summing Up**   181
Planning, Planning and Planning ▮ Keeping It All
Together ▮ The Power of the Family Business

Selected Bibliography   195
Suggested Readings

Sources of Assistance   199

Index   201

▮Checklists

Is Your Business Ready for Succession   17

Pre-Planning Analysis Checklist   50

Family Business Marketing Strategy Checklist   80

The Succession Planning Organizer   101

Succession Decisions Checklist   131

The Transition Management Checklist   157

The Letting Go Checklist   179

▌Introduction

This is a book for families in business who want to stay in business. It's for those who want to start planning for the continuity of business ownership and management by the next generation of their families and for those who are already into the process and aren't happy with how it's going. It's for the CEO in the executive tower, for the service station owner pumping gas in the rain, and for their sons and daughters. It's for people like Larry.

Larry is 40, and his company, Pro Machines, Inc., is a clear winner. Eleven years ago, Larry made a long-standing dream come true by starting his own high-tech machine tooling company, using money borrowed from a few friends, some optimistic relatives, and one very nervous banker. A lot of hard work followed—days, nights, and weekends spent sweating over the drafting table, the telephone, and the adding machine.

But now Pro Machines is doing over $20 million annually, riding the cutting edge of industry technology, and looking solid. Larry owns 74 percent of the company and is making more money than he ever imagined. He's enthusiastic about Pro Machines' long-range prospects and even considering diversification. Most of all, he's excited by the idea of his own kids coming into the company, eventually owning and running it, and keeping Pro Machines, Inc.—and his dream—alive into succeeding family generations. ▌

Larry's desire to see his company become a true family business is not unusual among entrepreneurs who have had the courage to step off into the unknown and then worked themselves silly to build a successful business. Among the many reasons why men and women take the risks and make the sacrifices necessary for business success is their need to be good providers, to give their families "the good life." They crave the satisfaction of creating with their own hands and minds the financial means for nice homes, vacations, education for the kids, the best of everything for those they love. Having scrambled to make it themselves, they dream of topping it all off by giving their children the best gift of all: a no-sweat start and a secure future. They dream of one day giving their sons and daughters the business.

For many business owners, the dream comes true. Thousands of thriving businesses in the United States are in the third and fourth generations of family ownership. They are headed by people who see the business not only as the source of a comfortable living but also as a focus of deep family pride and tradition. Many of these business owners have gone through some trying times in planning and managing the passing of ownership from one generation to the next. Others are running business organizations that still bear the family name but have no other resemblance to the companies founded by their parents or grandparents. While maintaining the continuity of a family business isn't always easy, most of the men and women who are doing it wouldn't have it any other way.

Of course, not all businesses survive their current owners. Some of them turn up their financial bellies and go quietly under. Others have founders who are textbook entrepreneurs, building a company only to sell it and build another; they have no interest in passing along a family business tradition. And many businesses are sold, merged, or liquidated when their owners want to transfer ownership and management to the next generation but somehow can't make the transition work.

What happens? In some cases, the business owner's family members just aren't interested in coming into the business and making a career of it. The manufacturer's son would rather sell real estate. The software developer's daughter opts for medicine. In other cases, the family has learned to enjoy the financial benefits of the business, but it hasn't developed much zest for the hard work and responsibility required to keep them flowing. Or sometimes when the owner's sons and daughters do come into the business, they turn out not to be competent managers. If the parent accepts that bitter truth in time, he or she gracefully puts the business to bed before retirement. If not, the business not so gracefully goes down the tubes.

In almost every case where a solid business is successfully handed over to the next generation of the owner's family, it's because the business owner has analyzed, planned, and managed the transfer of ownership. The business owner has planned thoroughly and far enough in advance to give succession at least an even chance. Not only has the owner put down firm groundwork for succession, but he or she has also allowed for those quirks of human nature that can wreck the implementation of even the best-laid plan. After analyzing the business, the family, and the chances that the two will make a good match, the owner puts together a sound succession strategy. For such companies, the change of management and ownership may not be perfectly smooth sailing but the company doesn't end up on the rocks, either.

If you are the founder or owner of a business, the son or daughter of a business owner, or otherwise closely related to a privately owned business, this book will provide you with a realistic view of the ins and outs of business ownership succession. The ideas and information here are supported by research in the social, psychological, and management sciences. They have been shaped by observations of families and their businesses and by the practical insights of numerous businesspersons, including the author.

This is a book about how you, as the owner of a business, can plan and carry out the transfer of your company to your children or other family members. It's also about how a prospective successor to a family business can prepare for future ownership and management. It is a step-by-step guide through a very complex, often frustrating, and sometimes heartbreaking process. The book looks at the good and bad experiences of business owners, successors, and families, analyzing their brilliant strokes and their great mistakes; it summarizes the lessons learned by others and suggests how they can be applied to planning for the continuity of your own family business.

This book is not about taxes or estate planning or getting your cash out of your company. It's about the people factors in ownership and management succession in the family business and how to deal with them. It's about how to keep a family business in the family—and keep the family in business.

A Family Affair

What Is a Family Business?

A family business is a business that is owned either wholly or in the majority by one person or by members of one family. It may be headed by its entrepreneur founder and employ a spouse or other relatives, or it may be owned and operated by the founder's children, grandchildren, or other family members. The family business may be organized as a proprietorship, a partnership, or a closely held corporation, or it may be publicly traded, with one family owning enough stock to maintain a controlling interest. The family business's distinguishing characteristic is that one family owns and operates it, directs its management, or exercises another form of control.

The family business is probably the oldest business form in human history. When our prehistoric ancestors gave up chasing mastodons across the plains and settled down on the riverbank to scratch a living from the soil, one member of the clan went into the brokering trade, swapping his clan's sweet potatoes for another clan's grain and brussels sprouts. The first time the clan trader persuaded the spouse and children to help schlepp the produce or operate the abacus at the checkout, family business was born. An illustrious history has followed, from Noah and Sons Nature Cruises, Inc., to the Gucci family's leather shops.

Today family business is big business in the United States. Approximately 90 percent of all American businesses are owned outright or controlled by families, and they generate more than 50 percent of the annual gross national product. Half of all the nonfarm private sector workers in this country are employed in family businesses. (One cynic has suggested that the other half works for the federal government.) Family-owned businesses range in size from mom-and-pop delicatessens to billion-dollar conglomerates. At last count, nearly 40 percent of the Fortune 500 companies were family owned or controlled.

Management Dream or Nightmare?

A family-owned company can be either the most flexible or the most cumbersome of business structures. When only a few family members share decision-making authority, a company can be aggressive in the marketplace and quickly respond to changes in the business environment. A well-oiled family business runs circles around its more diversely owned competitors. It may have better access to capital because of a long and cordial relationship with lending institutions. Perhaps it can also afford to take a longer than normal view of strategic planning because its stockholders may be willing to calculate their returns over generations instead of fiscal quarters. On the other hand, a family business that is unable to shake up shortsighted directors or come down on incompetent employees because "they're members of the family" is trying to figure-skate in a sleeping bag.

The Family's Mark on the Business

The family business is a unique business organization that integrates a business system with a fundamentally different family system. Generally speaking, a business system is organized to achieve specific goals, driven by tasks, and characterized by competitiveness. A family system is bound and motivated largely by traditional responsibilities and loyalties; it is characterized by unity. Meshing one system with the other inevitably means that many of the family's biases, quirks, and internal relationships will bleed through into the business's operating style, decision making, and future prospects. The O'Brien family provides an example of the impact this influence can have.

>Patrick and John O'Brien are first cousins who inherited equal ownership shares of O'Brien's Fresh Markets, Inc., a regional grocery chain, from their fathers. In 1968, ten years after they took over the business, the cousins nearly came to blows one night during a televised Nixon-Humphrey campaign debate. They haven't spoken to one another since. At family gatherings, Patrick and John stay at opposite ends of the room and sit at opposite ends of the table. Their families exchange Christmas gifts but with only the wives' and kids' names on them. The rest of the family regards them as lovable old cranks.

>At the office, John and Patrick communicate only through a secretary. "Ms. Jones, tell Mr. Liberal Democrat down the hall there that revenues at the Martinsville store are down eight percent this month, and ask him if inventory or employee cuts should be made, and if he says inventory ask him what product lines." John and Patrick have grudging respect for one another's management abilities. But since they don't have direct discussions, decisions are made with rapid exchanges of memos that the cousins address to one another by title but not name. When Patrick and John disagree, the one who generates the most paper in the shortest time usually wins. Vendors have to dash back and forth between the cousins' offices, making part of a presentation to John, another part to Patrick, then back to John for his decision on the order, and back to Patrick for a signature. Neither cousin will consider selling out to the other, the business continues to do very well, and the rest of the family can only wonder why. ∎

Family businesses tend to be deeply and devilishly personal. If a business is not the owners' paramour, as some entrepreneurs' spouses suspect, it is certainly his or her child. So the business owner may experience some wildly mixed emotions—a little like lending the new Jag to a teenager for his first prom—when he or she contemplates handing over the company, even to family members. Pride mixes with possessiveness, and the eagerness to see things go well for the next generation conflicts with terror of the consequences if they don't. Some owners treat handing over control of the business like giving up smoking. They know they need to do it, they say they want to do it, and yet they fight it every step of the way.

Even the coolest heads face some excruciating choices. Which person is best qualified to head the company? What will be the roles of other family members? What will happen to the loyal nonfamily employees? Transferring ownership authority and management responsibility to family members ought to be guided by sound business judgment, just as if the business were being sold to a stranger. But the prospect of ownership succession within a family sometimes clouds that judgment with contradictory loyalties and private preferences. When the owner's relationships with his or her family collide with devotion to the business, objectivity goes out the window and potentially destructive stresses can build up on all sides.

Finally, family businesses are surprisingly fragile. Few of them become thousand-year dynasties. In fact, according to Richard Beckhard and his associates at MIT, the average life expectancy of a family-owned business in the United States is only about 24 years, which coincides almost exactly with the length of time the average founder remains active in company management. Out of 100 family businesses in operation today, no more than 30 will pass successfully into the hands of their present owners' children.

Which Businesses Survive Succession . . . ?

What distinguishes the 30 businesses that make the transition into the next generation of ownership from the 70 that retire with their founders? What factors influence the probability of successful succession? Professor David Ambrose at the University of Nebraska at Omaha has identified several key characteristics of those businesses that survive family ownership succession.

▮ First, the surviving businesses are generally perceived by family members as *financially and organizationally sound*, profitable, and positioned solidly in their industries and their communities. Of at least equal importance, the businesses are also seen by the family as being satisfying, even fun, to own and operate and as a way to meet some of the psychological and emotional, as well as monetary, needs of living.

▮ The surviving family business is likely to be *a family affair*. Ideally, family members are employed in the business. At the very least, they are kept informed about the business, and they provide encouragement and moral support through its ups and downs. The family understands the business and accepts it as a natural adjunct to family life.

▮ The probability of continuity is higher when family members coming into the business get *prior training and experience* for ownership responsibilities and management jobs. Their training may include formal education in business administration or a relevant technical area, specialized seminars, experience elsewhere in the industry, or apprenticeship in the family company itself before they assume full responsibility and authority. The company is also more likely to avoid internal instability during and following a management change when incoming family members have a chance to earn their spurs and the respect of company employees instead of being handed the top jobs on a silver platter.

▮ The most crucial characteristic of the surviving family business is *flexible, forward-looking leadership*. Here, the present owner anticipates and accepts change that benefits the business. The chances of family business survival are dramatically improved when the owner has carried out thorough *analysis and long-range planning* in preparation for succession and when he or she actively manages and monitors the transition in a humane but businesslike fashion.

And Which Ones Don't?

The family businesses that do not survive are not only those that fail to meet Professor Ambrose's criteria for continuity.

They also include businesses that are distinguished by some definitely negative features.

■ The family business that does not survive is often one that the family views as *marginal* in revenues and profits, the efficiency of its management and operations, and its position in the market and the community. The company is a source of family tension instead of family pride, and if it is discussed around the house at all, the talk is hushed and ominous. The younger family members' low level of enthusiasm for joining the business is not hard to understand: Despite their family loyalties, few young people with other options are interested in starting life's long voyage in a leaky boat.

■ Succession may not succeed in the family business when there is overt *family pressure* on the upcoming generation to take over the business. "Daddy's old and tired and sick, but if he has to give up the company it'll break his heart. He's done so much for you. You've just got to come home and run the plumbing fixtures business—even if it means flushing your law practice." Usually nothing less than monumental guilt will force a young person to move into such a situation, and that's one of the worst possible motivations for a business career.

■ There's not much incentive for successors to a family business that makes little or *no allowance for nonbusiness needs* and interests. "The only way this company can be run is the way I've always run it: 16 hours a day, seven days a week, and no time off for sissy sports—like golf!" Young people are still willing to make money the old-fashioned way—by earning it—but not all of them are willing to sacrifice all other dimensions of their lives to do it. It's hard to sell a business with too many restrictive covenants—even to your own kids.

■ On the other hand, a company may not make it across the generation gap if the prospective successors see a future in the family business as *too easy and unchallenging*, a free ride on dear old Dad's coattails. A young person with the character and self-esteem necessary to manage a dynamic business will want to look a parent in the eye and say, "You had to be smart and you had to be tough to build this company, but I have to be just as smart and just as tough to keep it going and growing." If such a statement is not possible or is obviously not true, the younger person may not consider the family business to be worth his or her time and talent. It's a kind of macho stance that sons and daughters alike sometimes take because they naturally need to prove themselves as successful adults and businesspersons in their own eyes and in the eyes of their parents.

■ Even family businesses that make it over other hurdles tend to get into trouble if the senior generation *won't let go.* "I know I promised to make you CEO of this company, but I don't think you're ready for it yet. I'm just gonna stick around until you figure out what's going on—if you ever do." It makes good sense for a business owner to be cautious when transferring power and to remain interested in the company that has been his or her life's work. But keeping successors waiting in the wings too long can convey everything from a lack of confidence in their management potential to contempt for them as responsible adults. Some retired CEOs try to drive their companies from the backseat even after they've supposedly handed over control. If the backseat driving is necessary, then somebody has done a very sloppy job of selecting and preparing the new generation of executives. When it is unnecessary, it can be destructive to the new generation's management effectiveness and morale and, ultimately, to the business itself.

■ Finally, it is almost always true that family businesses do not survive when there has been *no planning for succession.* "I've decided to retire at the end of the year, and guess what! You and your brother are gonna take over the company. Come on down to the plant Monday morning and pick out your new office." The successor who willingly steps into business ownership and management with no planning and preparation is in serious trouble from day one, and the founder or owner who lets it happen might as well kiss a lifetime's work goodbye.

Figure 1.1 summarizes the factors that can influence succession in the family business.

Why Succession Either Sails or Sinks

The greatest threats to the continuity of the family business are not estate taxes, laws governing corporations, or the mechanics of stock transfers. The greatest threats are the nature of family relationships—among siblings, between spouses, and between generations—and the personality of the founder or senior owner of the company.

FIGURE 1.1. Factors Influencing the
              Probability of Successful
              Succession

	High Probability	**Low Probability**
Owner-Driven	Sound and profitable business Business satisfying to run Flexible, forward-looking leadership Analysis/planning for succession	Marginal business Pressure on family members No allowance for nonbusiness needs No planning for succession Retiring owner won't let go
Family-Driven	Family members work in the business Family knowledgeable and supportive Family successors trained and experienced	Business appears unchallenging

Handing over control of a business has financial and power implications for everyone involved. Like the parceling out of a fat estate, it can bring old rivalries and resentments to the surface and give a new focus to long-simmering disputes. When succession within the family fails and takes a solid and profitable business down with it, the real cause can most often be traced to underlying difficulties in family relationships and a failure to take those difficulties into account when analyzing and planning for the transfer of power.

Beyond the Second Generation

If only 30 percent of family-owned businesses survive into the second generation, how many pass intact into the hands of the family's third generation, the grandchildren or other relatives of the founder? National statistics show that fewer than 15 of 100 companies will end up being successfully managed by a founding family's third generation. Some interesting and instructive—and sometimes sad—things happen to the rest. Here's an illustration.

In the early 1930s, young Walter Hocker found a job in a small department store in Fulton, Missouri, to supplement his income from an inherited farm. The store steadily lost ground during those Depression years, and as it was about to go under, Walter bought it, using the farm as a down payment. With hard work, a sharp pencil, and talents for clever buying and pricing, Walter made a success of the little store in Fulton and of the 11 much larger ones that he opened around the country over the next 25 years.

After growing up in retail merchandising, Walter's children became successful company owners and managers when he retired. As the second generation took hold, annual revenues broke $50 million, and Walter's family chain of department stores was becoming a corporate institution. But Walter's otherwise sound ownership succession plan contained what might be called a Santa Claus Flaw: the distribution of a substantial number of shares in the company through direct gifts and trusts to Walter's minor grandchildren and in-laws. Walter's own children received enough of the voting stock for control—but just barely.

A few third-generation family members went to work in the business. Many more who didn't were given stock nevertheless, but because they weren't active in the company, they had no commitment to it as a family enterprise. They developed a real taste for regularly paid dividends, however, and they began to think that larger dividends or fat cash-outs would be even tastier. In Walter's declining years, the corporate boardroom began to look like the parliament of a small country, with everyone making deals and switching allegiances in order to be closer to the head of the line when the goodies were passed out.

When the last of Walter's children retired from the corporation in 1983, the business began to come apart. The four grandchildren and two nephews who ended up with the majority interest in the company spent most of their time in court, suing and countersuing one another. They suspended hostilities only long enough to vote together for corporate buy-backs of their stock. One by one the stores have been sold to pay for their shenanigans. Before the end of this year, the last of the chain, the little flagship store in Fulton, will go on the block. ∎

In the case of Walter Hocker, it was the founder's own generous but shortsighted impulses that ultimately sank both his dream and a profitable family business. Walter spent most of his life at the very center of the company, never looking up to analyze either the prospects for the business's continuity or the needs and characteristics of his family. He lit the fuse on a disaster by failing to link his heirs' contributions to the business with their enjoyment of its benefits. Walter also didn't take into account a critical premise in succession planning: Owning a family company and running it are two distinctly different things. He left his own sons and daughters without the healthy margin of ownership control that should have gone along with their management responsibilities.

By the time the members of the third generation began to wield ownership power, Walter's company was a sprawling and, for most of them, impersonal corporation, just a big department store chain in which they owned a lot of stock. Because they were so far removed from the challenge and satisfaction of running it, his descendents felt no more compunction about taking the business apart than would a gang of corporate raiders. The only good news is that Walter didn't live to see his company die in its fifty-fifth year.

The heirs of tobacco magnate R. J. Reynolds provided a more recent front-page illustration of this phenomenon. During the 1989–1990 fight among corporate management, the board of directors, and innumerable Wall Street investment bankers over the leveraged buy-out of RJR/Nabisco, one member of the far-flung Reynolds' clan tried to raise a family effort to rescue the company that his grandfather had built. Smith Bagley couldn't even get his relatives' attention because they were too busy watching the price of their stock being bid up.

Will the Family and the Business Mix?

In the best of worlds, owning and operating a family business ought to be a family affair, and passing it along to the next generation ought to be fulfilling for all concerned. But both families and businesses are complex and unpredictable organisms. People in families—parents and children, brothers and sisters—usually relate to one another in ways that are not necessarily best for people in businesses to relate to one another. Behavior that is accepted with a shrug around the kitchen table can be intolerable around the conference table. In a business setting, supervisors and subordinates, and CEOs and junior partners, routinely make demands on one another that would tear many modern families to shreds.

A succession process that either transforms an entrepreneurial business into a family business or extends family business ownership into the next generation can accentuate both the strengths and the vulnerabilities of the family and the business. By mixing business dynamics with family dynamics, succession may produce new family stresses and throw a company into chaos, or it may form some very successful relationships among family members and carry the company to a new performance plateau.

To succeed, ownership and management succession must include pre-planning analysis, developing a succession plan, managing the ownership transfer, monitoring the transition, and finishing cleanly when the retiring owner hands over control. In this entire process, the factor that most often makes the crucial difference is the comprehensiveness and quality of succession planning that the business owner is willing to do. The predictors of which family businesses will survive succession and which ones won't are not infallible. But they provide pretty strong evidence that while good planning by itself may not guarantee a long and happy life for the family business, it boosts the odds so dramatically that no family in business can afford to pass it up.

Is Your Business Ready for Succession?

This self-assessment is designed to help you begin thinking about family ownership and management succession in your business. For each of the following, circle the number that most nearly describes how you feel about the statement:

1 = *Strongly Agree*   3 = *Disagree*
2 = *Agree*   4 = *Strongly Disagree*

1. The founder or senior owner of a company is the one who knows the company best and should make all final decisions about its operation.   1 2 3 4

2. The only way to learn a job is by trial and error.   1 2 3 4

3. Successive generations seldom run the company as well as its founder did.   1 2 3 4

4. It isn't necessary to plan for succession in the family business if the current owner has only one child.   1 2 3 4

5. Planning for ownership and management succession is dangerous because it keeps everyone on edge for too long.   1 2 3 4

6. A business owner's family should be told of the business's successes but not its problems.   1 2 3 4

7. Younger family members should be brought into the owner's company in top positions so that employees will respect their authority.   1 2 3 4

8. Company employees should have little or no role in planning for succession in the business.   1 2 3 4

9. Planning for succession should not begin until the current owner is ready to retire.   1 2 3 4

10. A successful business owner's sons and   1 2 3 4
    daughters have a natural obligation to take ——————
    over the business.

      Total of all numbers circled

A total score of 40 on this self-assessment, indicating strong disagreement with every statement, shows your readiness to begin planning for family succession in your business. A score above 30 shows good orientation for succession planning. If your score is between 24 and 30, you should reconsider your views on family involvement in the business. If your score is 23 or below, pay very close attention to the next seven chapters of this book.

Analyzing the Factors and Estimating the Odds

Before making any major business move, the good manager first analyzes all the factors that are likely to affect the outcome and then estimates the chances of success or failure. A thorough analysis is particularly important in preparing for ownership succession in the family business because it can make the difference between a general plan that looks good in a management manual and a specific one that promotes ownership continuity of *this* business by *this* family. Because analysis can be so demanding, however, business owners overlook or ignore this step more often than any other component in the entire succession process. Here's what can happen if they do.

Roger was the owner and CEO of a $30 million company that distributes commercial cleaning products, selling tank cars full of solvents, tons of cleansers, and enough liquid soap to float the average armada. Roger had built a successful business in a competitive industry, and he had enough long-term contracts to stay in gravy for another ten years.

But at 48, Roger began to feel he had already done a respectable lifetime's worth of work, and early retirement was an appealing prospect. He started thinking seriously about bringing his two sons into the business and eventually handing it, and a secure future, over to them. During high school the boys had spent every summer and most holidays working for Roger. In college they seemed to like the idea of coming into the business full time after graduation. In fact, the older son began to talk about getting a graduate degree in business. Roger rushed to put together a succession plan that would transfer ownership to his sons and divide the responsibilities of running the company.

A couple of years later, however, the older son, still professing an interest in the business, enrolled in an MBA program to major in banking and finance. The younger one chose to get a little more experience before going into business. He joined the campus ROTC unit, which dressed him up in a snappy uniform and stuck him with a three-year postgraduate military obligation. The boys were looking less and less like future cleaning products distributors every day. Still, skippering his own boat through the Bahamas while collecting dividends from the company that bore his name sounded awfully good to Roger. So he held off the food conglomerate that wanted to buy him out and dreamed of sitting on his poop deck while his sons sat in the executive chairs.

Roger's older son went on to Wall Street and the younger one set off to see the world through U.S. Navy portholes. After two marriages, the younger son came home and joined the business. It was quite a few years later than Roger had planned when his son was finally ready to take over the company. At 70, Roger got in a little sailing after all. ∎

Roger's dream of continuing a family-owned business almost fell through, even though he made many sound preparations for a successful succession. He introduced his sons to the business when they were young, developed a succession plan, and prepared himself psychologically to hand over the management of his company. But he left out the crucial first step. He did not carefully analyze his company, his family, and himself, a step that might have helped him either to proceed differently with his succession planning or to see right up front the kind of trouble he would have making a match between his company and his family. Roger's experience shows the value of persistence. It also emphasizes that the whole purpose of analyzing the factors and estimating the odds is to lay the groundwork for a solid succession plan and to avoid surprises and setbacks later.

To analyze means to take apart an existing or prospective situation to look at its various components, formulating a set of specific questions, digging for information, and then interpreting the practical significance of the answers. Analyzing the prospects for family business succession requires a detailed examination of the business, the successors, and even the current owner and chief executive. When all the data have been collected, decisions have to be made about if, and then how, the business can be confidently handed over to members of the family who can run it successfully. If the analysis has been honest and complete, there may be a few uncomfortable answers and some unhappy conclusions to deal with, and it might be necessary to draw up a succession plan that differs slightly from the one everyone expected. On the whole, though, most people would prefer the discomfort of rearranging some expectations now to the misery of watching their businesses fall apart later.

Before Analysis

If the analysis of the business, the family, and the owner is going to be anything more than an interesting exercise, a few questions must be answered before it is started: *Is continuity of family ownership of this business really important? To whom is it important? And why?* The obvious and most satisfying answers are, yes, it is important. It's important to the owner because it's a solid business that has taken hard work to build, and it's important to the owner's family because it means good careers and financial security for their futures. It can also be important to the company's employees and their families for the same reasons. Depending on the size of the business, its continuity could even be important to the economic well-being of an entire community. All of these may be compelling reasons for owners to push for family ownership continuity of their businesses.

Of course, the answers might be different. Maybe continuity is important to the owner because those big warehouses on the skyline, the family name on the front door, or a portrait on the boardroom wall would be monuments to his or her success. Very few people who are motivated to build a business are free from needing some such assurance of immortality, and there's nothing wrong with that.

But at the same time, the business's continuity may not be perceived by the owner's family members as all that important to their future security, especially if they have other career options or if the sale or merger of the company would give them a windfall in short-term cash or long-term dividends. If there is no significant shortage of jobs or economic diversity in the community, the business's employees and neighbors might prefer other options, including the continuing operation of the company by a new owner. Or maybe the company's technology and product viability have finally peaked, and saving it from extinction would be unreasonably expensive. Perhaps changes in the community's economic base—from heavy manufacturing to soft industry, for example—or in its tax treatment of commercial enterprises are squeezing the company's kind of business out of the mainstream. Under such conditions, passing along the company to the upcoming generation would be a real disservice, one for which an owner might be remembered as the person who hung the millstone around the family's neck.

So determining how important it is that a business continue under family ownership, and why, is more than a just review of the current owner's personal preferences. The justification for continuity needs to be examined critically and questions need to be asked to get at some practical long-range truth. If this probing produces serious doubts, then maybe continuity of family ownership would be a no-win situation. Putting the business to bed when the owner is ready to retire could actually be in everybody's best interest. But if continuity of business ownership within the family is equally important to the owner and to the prospective successors, then it is time to push ahead.

Analyzing the Business

Although analyzing the business for prospects of continuity is complicated, it is also valuable because it helps to organize an understanding of the company in terms that can be applied to succession planning. Some parts of the analysis can be left to specialists, but other parts must be done by the owner alone. Table 2.1 summarizes each aspect of analyzing the business.

First, the owner and the accountants should prepare a complete *financial analysis* focused on the company's present strengths and weaknesses and on its long-term financial prospects. The numbers must be scrutinized, and that's a job that some owners, especially owners of smaller businesses, resist for the same reason they resist going to the doctor for a mysterious pain: They're afraid of what they might find out. The analysis should focus on asset values, revenues, cash flow, and overhead—both current and projected. The company's system of financial controls needs special attention. Is it outmoded? If the company's growth suddenly accelerated, would the financial controls stand up to a significant boost in inventory or receivables? Growth is a real hazard for some smaller businesses simply because their financial controls are not adequate to keep up with it.

The next step is a thorough and objective analysis of the company's current *strategic position* and its projected position for at least the next ten years. The company's market position, and its production, sales and service plans, and capacities should be reviewed by the owner, perhaps with help from a consultant or outside expert. Where is the company headed, and what course has been charted to get it there? Does the long-term strategy still make as much sense as it once did? If it doesn't, what will it take to change it? Regardless of the size of the business, this strategic analysis shouldn't be based on an assumption that the current CEO will continue as the chief mover and shaker. After all, the whole idea is to look at what the company is likely to do with someone else in charge.

There are generally accepted formats and standards and a lot of qualified help available for preparing those financial and strategic analyses. But the next stage, analyzing the character of the company, has to be done by the owner.

An individual's character comprises many traits—industriousness, initiative, resiliency, ethics, priorities, faults, and others. These are the factors that motivate an individual's behavior—that make the person tick—and constitute the substance that lies beneath the exterior. Consciously or unconsciously, everyone is constantly sizing up the character of their business

TABLE 2.1 Analyzing the Business

Financial and Strategic Analysis	Character Analysis	Long-Term Needs Analysis
Current cash flow and overhead Projected cash flow and overhead Financial controls system Current market position Projected market position (ten years) Current production/sales/service systems Projected production/sales/service systems	What kind of business is this? What makes it work? What are the company's problems, basic and transient, and how are they handled?	How far has the company come, and why? Where should the company be in 20 years? What kind of management will the company need to get there?
Bottom Line: How strong is this company, and how strong would it be with different management?	**Bottom Line:** What is the character or organic nature of this company?	**Bottom Line:** How far has this company come, what has it needed in the past, and what will it need in the future?

associates and friends. Character analysis is a key tool in anticipating how other people will react to conditions and demands in their immediate or universal environment. A business's character can be similarly analyzed, and the results are important because they help predict how the business will react to changing business conditions, including a change in ownership and management. Consider the following questions:

What Kind of Business Is This?

There are no simple answers here such as "It hauls freight" or "It makes horse collars." An analysis of the company's character should define what the company *is*, not what it *does*. Start by restating the company's goals. Then list the operating priorities that help to achieve those goals, including items like meeting delivery deadlines, servicing accounts fully and cheerfully, or taking care of employees, as well as making a decent profit.

What Makes This Company Work Successfully?

The owner who is intensely involved in the operation of his or her business may have to take a few mental steps back to get the full picture of what makes the company work. The most useful answers will be neither simple nor obvious, nor will they be limited to what can be seen from the boss's desk. What is important to know is how the company works on the inside and how it appears from the outside. Answers will have to be found to questions like these:

■ What is the production, sales, and service philosophy of the company, and how is it demonstrated by management and by employees?

■ What are the key internal relationships and loyalties that make the company function smoothly and productively? Among executives and managers? Between management and the directors? Between management and the employees? Among employees?

■ How do the employees view the company and its management, and how satisfied are they to be working at the company?

■ Does management promote a teamwork approach to getting the company's work done, or is the company's decision-making structure more vertical or compartmentalized?

▮ How much work do people in the company actually do? On the average, how many hours weekly does each category of employee work? How many hours weekly do the CEO and senior managers work? What time do they start and stop each day? How many of those working hours generate hard products—management memos as well as widgets—and how many generate plans and ideas?

▮ What is the company's real attitude toward its customers (all of them, not just the big spenders) and in what ways is it demonstrated? How does the typical customer or client perceive the company, and what's the evidence of that perception?

▮ What three or four things distinguish the company from other companies in its industry and from other businesses in its market and its community?

After these questions have been sorted out, list the ten most important answers. Then stop to think for a moment about which of those questions could be answered completely differently without seriously damaging the continued success of the business. This exercise should generate a little insight into how the character of the company could be affected by a change in its management, even within the family.

What Are the Company's Problems?

This calls for an honest and detailed appraisal of the company's negative characteristics and current or potential risks. List the liabilities of which only the owner is aware, along with those that are commonly known within the company or in the industry or community. The problems may include:

▮ Chronic or periodic constrictions in cash flow

▮ Deferred maintenance, upgrading, or expansion due to a capital shortage

▮ Uncomfortably wide seasonal swings in sales

▮ Minor but chronic employee goldbricking or theft

▮ Marginally competent senior managers

▮ Too many outlets removed from the distribution network

▮ Not enough modern marketing expertise in sales

- Competitive price-cutting that the company can't match
- Sexual harassment of lower-level employees by managers
- Impending government regulations that may increase costs of production or personnel
- Some board members starting to rebel

Which Problems Are Basic and Which Are Transient?

Basic problems are those that are characteristic of the industry or market. Solutions may be possible, affordable, or not, but in any case the problems have not been solved yet. Transient problems are those that can be dealt with by making changes in company personnel, policies, or procedures, acting on foreseeable twists and turns in the business environment, or just leaving them alone. All of the problems that a company faces and how it resolves them are elements of its character. They must be accounted for to understand the company's prospects for continuing as a family business.

How Far has This Company Come Since It Started, and What has Helped or Hindered Its Growth?

To measure the company's growth in terms of revenues, numbers of employees, asset value, and other key indicators, use simple arithmetic to get the rate of average annual growth. Calculate this in absolute terms and hard numbers, not just in glossy percentages. The results are for private analysis, not investors. As each year's changes are calculated, list those events, people, contracts, or sales breakthroughs that were especially important to the company, either positively or negatively. Then try to determine if these factors have made permanent marks on the company's character, and, if so, in what ways and why.

Where Should This Company Be in Twenty Years, and What Kind of Management Will it Need to Get There?

If 20 years is too long, pick a more realistic period. But make the longest projection possible while not overlooking more immediate goals that can, or must, be achieved in the interim. Consider the long-term possibilities of diversification, technological retooling, improved market share, growth or downsizing, a different organization or structure, new locations. Dream a little, but balance a vision of the future with the realities revealed in the earlier financial and strategic analyses.

Also, don't forget *where* the company is and *what* it is right now in terms of the operating characteristics and the problems identified earlier. What kind of ground will the company have to cover in order to stay healthy and dynamic as it moves 20 years into the future? What skills, attitudes, and orientation will be required of management during the next 20 years to build on the business's current strengths and to whittle down its deficits? This is another point where making a simple but complete list will be helpful. Enter a column of 20-year goals down one side of a page and the corresponding management requirements for accomplishing them down the other side.

The end product of analyzing the business should be a multidimensional view of the company's current character and the kind of management it needs to continue as a strong business operation. It should produce a clear, perhaps a new and even somewhat surprising, understanding not only of the company's financial and mechanical nature, but also of its organic nature, its character. Now it's time to focus the analytical microscope on the family to see if its members are capable of succeeding to ownership and management of the business.

Analyzing the Family

This step will probably be more difficult than analyzing the business because most people find it harder to be objective about their families than about their businesses. But this analysis must be done if succession decisions are going to hold up over the long haul.

What Kind of Family Is This?

Humorist Robert Benchley said that there are two types of people in this world: those who divide people into two types and those who don't. It's possible to go Benchley one better by describing a family as a working system that may fall into one of three types: (1) the interdependent family, (2) the independent family, or (3) the coherent family. Table 2.2 summarizes the characteristics of each type of family. Each type is subject to innumerable exceptions and variations, as are most broad categories of facts or people or objects. But these types suggest some important distinctions among family groups that may bear upon their prospects as successful owners and operators of a family business.

Members of the *interdependent family* tend to be very sensitive to one another's needs, interests, and preferences. The family usually describes itself and is described by others as close-knit. Family members show a great deal of concern for one another's well-being. They may also rely on each other's opinions to guide their own behavior. They share friends, or at least they approve of one another's friends. They make few personal or family decisions—from who Judy dates for the high school dance to where the family goes for this year's vacation—without reaching some kind of family consensus. A strongly interdependent family may view the rest of the world as somewhat threatening and keep its wagons in a tight circle as a defense against a hostile social environment.

The interdependent family that owns and operates a business can achieve a remarkable degree of decision-making uniformity and management maneuverability. Every member of the family, whether employed in the business or not, feels involved in its operations. As a family enterprise, the business is a focus of family interest and tends to have the solid support of family members. Seldom do prolonged hassles or polarized opinions get in the way of running the family company. On the other hand, such strong family unity may make nonfamily employees of the company feel shut out of decision-making processes. So the interdependent business family sometimes finds itself pitted against, rather than working with, its own employees.

The *independent family*, by contrast, sometimes seems to be a small group of individuals who just happen to have the same last name. Family members demonstrate highly individualistic preferences, tastes, and personal goals. Each one lives in his or her own corner of the world and marches to a different drummer, drawing support and stimulation from relationships outside the family. There are few internal rules, except the ones necessary for disciplining children and otherwise maintaining basic order. Internal communication is weak, and internal com-

TABLE 2.2 What Kind of Family Is It?

Family Type	Relationships Characteristics	Implications for Business Ownership Positive	Negative
Interdependent	Close-knit, sensitive to one another's needs and opinions; shares values, priorities, even friends	Total involvement in the business; uniformity in decision making; few family disputes	Strong unity shuts out non-family employees; may become indecisive, lose touch with business environment
Independent	Highly individualistic and competitive members, insensitive to one another's needs, opinions, values; members relate more to outsiders than to others in family	Authoritative, even dictatorial management style; may produce exceptionally capable individual leaders	Frequent disagreements; disruptive behavior can lead to fragmented interests and business collapse
Coherent	Balance between internal and external relationships, between individuality and cohesion; family effective as group	Effective but not rigid management style; good environment for discussion and consensus on family and business decisions	May become too dependent on consensus, too self-conscious for business decisiveness

petitiveness, between parents and children and among siblings, is strong. Decisions are made and actions are taken by individuals with little concern for the opinions of other family members, and family consensus is almost never sought. Judy dates whomever she damned well pleases, and if three members of the family decide to vacation at Yellowstone, the others may go to Nassau instead.

Most independent families that successfully run businesses do so in one of two ways. Either one member of the family has indisputable decision-making authority over the company, with the other members acquiescent, ignorant, or unconcerned, or there is a one person–one vote power platform, where the majority rules on every decision and there's no provision for veto or appeal. Even in these situations, members of the independent family may pursue individual policy or management agendas, embrace the causes of disgruntled employees or social movements that conflict with the company's interests, or string out the resolution of important business decisions. But the independent family sometimes produces one or two brilliant individuals whose initiative and leadership benefit the company and its family owners far more profoundly than would a management consensus on every issue.

The *coherent family*, to borrow words from Peter Davis of the Wharton School of Business, "tends to balance each member's outside needs with the family need for cohesion." The family unit is flexible enough to accept each member's individuality but strong enough to provide mutual support. Each member may have distinct views and enjoy rewarding relationships outside the family and bring home a variety of perspectives to family interactions. But everyone hangs together when the family confronts key issues. In the coherent family, members are effective as individuals, and the family is effective as a group.

The impact of family coherence on the operation of a family-owned company is generally positive. Management is effective but not rigid or monolithic. The family is sensitive to employee concerns and prepared for necessary changes in business policies or strategies. There is usually a healthy balance between the family's interests and the company's interests, even if the two are financially intertwined. If one member of the family moves to the company's top job, it is almost always as a result of constructive family discussion and with the other members' endorsement and support.

Extremes of Behavior

There is nothing in these categories that distinguishes one type of family as "normal" and another type as "pathological." Well-balanced, successful business families may be interdependent, independent, or coherent. It is when a family slips into extremes of behavior that problems can develop in its business. For example, if members of the interdependent family become totally enmeshed in one another's lives, the family can become so inwardly focused that its ability to interact effectively with the outside world is impaired. The totally interdependent family may soon find itself isolated and unable to comprehend and respond to the realities of its social and business environments. The family's ability to concentrate on business management is increasingly eroded, and the company may wallow and sink. On the other hand, members of extremely independent families may ultimately cease to relate to one another at all, give up shared values and internal loyalties, and stop functioning as a family unit altogether. Family members' individual interests and rivalries may consume the attention of the family company, which sooner or later falls into chaos and collapses.

Even the coherent family can have trouble running its business if it becomes too self-conscious. Whoever is supposed to be in charge starts to lose his or her grip, and a misguided attempt at democracy in action replaces rational management decision making. "Shoot, we're a coherent family, aren't we? So if you kids think we should liquidate half the company assets to pay cash for those laundromats in Hong Kong, why that's just what we'll do!" There are times when a balanced family perspective is no substitute for hard-nosed control of corporate actions.

Understanding how a family works as a system—interdependently, independently, or coherently—provides a context for sorting out which family members are best equipped to meet a company's current and future needs. Again, the idea is to make the most objective assessments possible. The analysis of the family should not be limited to the owner's children. To get the broadest view of where the family talent lies, the analysis should include nephews and nieces, sons and daughters-in-law, cousins, and others.

Analyzing Skills and Abilities

A 1989 *Wall Street Journal* survey of business owners found that their strongest motivation in planning the allocation of business responsibilities and rewards among their children was a desire to be fair. An oldest son may be bright, personable, and yet unable to plan his way through a change of socks. A daughter may be a dynamo with not a shred of business sense. But *to be fair*, the business owner insists, the son deserves first crack at heading the company because he's a people person who could inspire loyalty and productivity—and he is, after all, the first son. And daughter should have her share of company ownership and management decision making simply because she *is* the daughter.

These are not the answers that will best serve a business owner in analyzing family members' capacities for company management and leadership. First it should be determined where the basic management skills are in the family, based on observable behavior. Who shows the greatest ability to plan logically to achieve specific goals? Who has the capacity for vision? Who makes the best decisions—the one who digs out relevant information, lines up the pros and cons on an issue, anticipates the outcomes of various options, and then takes a position and follows through? Who is most willing to allocate time and resources and to work hard?

The politics of being the second-generation head of a family-owned business could give a Chicago ward boss a bleeding ulcer. So it's also helpful to analyze individual family members' natural aptitudes for the diplomacy that will be required to keep peace in the family while simultaneously running the company. Who most often seems to satisfy other family members' needs while getting where he or she wants to go—without revealing the iron hand in the velvet glove? Which family members would age well in senior executive positions in the company, maintaining family loyalty, support, and cohesiveness over time? Who is coming along as a family leader?

Matching Capabilities With Needs

When each family member's management skills and qualities of diplomatic leadership have been considered, his or her capabilities should be compared to the company's specific characteristics and needs. If the company's work gets done by teams of managers, supervisors, and employees, who in the family is a good team player, with a flair for team building and team leadership? If the company functions as a hierarchy, who has a commanding personality and can also delegate responsibility with clear instructions, maintain management oversight through a few lieutenants, and stay aware of a complex organization through reports and other indirect means? If good customer relations has been identified as one of the prime reasons for the company's success, which person is potentially the best human relations strategist? If the company does a lot of business with government agencies, who has the aptitude for untangling obtuse procurement specifications and working with layers of bureaucracy?

Analyzing Direct Experience

Now ask some hard-core questions about direct experience:

■ Who in the family knows the business best at this time?

■ Which family members have worked in the company and in what jobs?

■ Who has made a point of learning how the company functions and why?

■ Who has experience in the industry, either directly (in another company) or tangentially (perhaps as a lawyer, technical consultant, or labor arbitrator)?

If any family members have outside experience directly related to their prospective successor roles, their track records in those jobs should be checked. There are, of course, professional executives who move successfully from one corporate presidency to another. But an owner who is planning to recruit the company's next management corps from among family members should very carefully analyze the relevance of family members' experiences to the company's particular character and needs.

Analyzing Management Development Needs

Once the family members with basic skills, natural aptitudes, and personal characteristics that match the company's requirements have been identified, consider what training and experience would be needed to shape potential candidates into the best prepared new owners and executives. The information collected and the conclusions reached at this stage can be used later in planning the next generation's participation in ownership and in making the critical selection of the family member who will follow as the next head of the company. Here's an example.

> *Dana, the wife of Bob's only son, has worked for the past three years as assistant comptroller of Bob's company. Dana is an MBA/CPA and a capable financial manager, and she shows a lot of additional leadership potential. Over lunch earlier this year, Dana told Bob of her strong interest in remaining with the company and offered some sound new ideas for improving operations, productivity, and profits. Even though she's a relative by marriage and not by blood, Dana is trusted and respected by the other members of the family. Bob is starting to think that Dana might be a good choice for the presidency when he retires.* ∎

But how far is Dana from being ready for the company's top job? Do her proven skills in financial management qualify her to run the entire company, or is she too one-dimensional? Does she have technical or personal deficits that could hinder her from taking and exercising CEO responsibility? Would additional training to broaden and sharpen her executive abilities bring her up to speed, or has she reached the peak of her professional development? If more training would be useful, what kind of training would be best and where can she get it? What else would Dana need in order to become a competent chief executive who inspires confidence not only in the employees but also in the rest of the family?

An analysis of specific family members' management development needs is important because running a business has become a much larger and more complex job than it was 50, or even 20, years ago. Grandpa may have had no formal management training before launching his shipping line, but that was back before regulation and litigation became commonplace in the business world. Today there are very few natural-born CEOs—even among young people who have grown up in the business and gotten good basic educations—who are ready to assume top management authority and responsibility without some kind of focused program of preparation. Identifying gaps in prospective successors' knowledge, skills, and experience and looking for ways to fill them are key tasks in preparing to hand over a company to the next generation.

Analyzing Nonbusiness Needs

The next step in the family analysis, examining family members' important nonbusiness needs and how the company can help to meet them, may seem like a waste of time to some business owners. "Who the hell cares what the kid's interests are outside the office? This is a business, not a social club." That's a point well taken, and if the next CEO will be hired in the open market, his or her needs and preferences should be adjusted to the company's requirements, not vice versa.

But that attitude won't help if the goal is to perpetuate ownership and management of the business within the family. A later chapter of this book looks at some of the reasons why people choose not to follow their parents in business. At this point, suffice it to say that the American national experience of the 1960s had quite an impact on the old-fashioned work ethic. Contemporary young people often view work and leisure as related but clearly separate dimensions of their lives. With considerable backing from psychological research, they see leisure as necessary if they are to maintain their focus and performance in work activities. Many of them are not as willing as their parents were to sacrifice personal interests—relationships with their own spouses and children, as well as time for themselves—to make a buck.

So, consider each family member's nonbusiness needs when analyzing if or how well he or she would function in company ownership and management. It's important to be aware of prospective successors' personal interests. Do they like sports or other physical recreation? Getting away to a vacation house? Attending cultural events? Belonging to clubs that are purely social or recreational? Writing or speaking for business or nonbusiness groups? Hobbies? Spending long weekends or other quality time with their families? How much time and energy do they devote to such activities, and how do they rank them? For the business owner who has never thought about family members' personal interests, now is a good time to start.

Be thoughtful in correlating family members' nonbusiness needs with the company's management needs. Can the company run successfully without crushing the nonbusiness interests of well-qualified future family owners and managers? Maybe a 70-hour executive week is an essential management requirement of the business. If so, the successor search should be concentrated on the family's dyed-in-the-wool workaholics. It's just possible, though, that a 70-hour week is the present CEO's personal preference or a habit held over from the company's demanding but exhilarating start-up days. Maybe the company really doesn't need that many hours from a competent CEO today—or, if it does, then maybe it's time to overhaul the management system.

Either way, careful attention should be paid to how business and nonbusiness interests coexist in the lives of the owner's potential successors and how life inside the company can allow for life outside the company. This factor will have to be accounted for when the owner develops and markets a succession plan. Also, this step in the analysis may uncover a refreshing perspective for the current CEO's own use when retirement from active management approaches.

Wrapping Up the Family Analysis

The important thing in analyzing the fit between the family and the business is to be as thorough and as objective as possible. (Table 2.3 breaks out the components and fundamental questions for the complete family analysis.) Business owners can still love their family members and admire their many wonderful qualities while admitting that their management potential is not exactly unlimited. If that's the case, a family member's best career option might lie in the company's technical or sales divisions, rather than in the executive suite, or perhaps they would be happier in another company or even in another profession.

Or with luck, family analysis might uncover a true unpolished gem, a really bright prospect for management leadership in the family business. In any case, both the family and the company will be stronger and happier later if time is taken now to identify how well family members and company needs mesh and to plan accordingly.

Analyzing the Owner

Studies in the sociology and psychology of family business succession confirm that in most cases the largest measure of credit for a successful transfer of ownership and management goes to the founder, owner, or senior family member in the business. Likewise, when a succession effort unravels, the foun-

TABLE 2.3 Analyzing the Family

Family Type	Individual Abilities and Characteristics	Development Needed	Family Nonbusiness Needs	Successor Prospects
Interdependent	Basic management skills	Skills training	Family commitment	Good CEO?
Independent	Leadership and diplomacy	Broader experience	Recreation	Good in another position?
Coherent	Abilities related to company characteristics: —team player/leader —command personality —human relations —client tolerance Directly relevant experience	Personal development	Personal time Other priorities	Not good for your company?
Bottom Line: Is this family type suited for business ownership/management?	**Bottom Line:** Are there capabilities in the family to company needs?	**Bottom Line:** What are the further development needs of family members, and can they be met?	**Bottom Line:** What are family members' nonbusiness needs, and can the business meet them?	**Bottom Line:** Who's qualified, and for what?

der or owner is usually at the center of the problem. So a complete succession analysis includes a careful examination of the succession readiness of the current owner of the business in his or her roles as entrepreneur, executive, and family leader.

Analyzing the family is tougher than analyzing the business, but self-analysis is the toughest part of the process yet. Audiologists know that we never hear our own voices as others hear them because of how sound resonates inside our heads. For much the same reason, it's hard to be objective about ourselves: Our self-perceptions resonate psychologically and emotionally inside our own heads. We may exaggerate our positive and negative traits, excessively justify our past actions, or make unrealistic projections of our future behavior. Even so, an owner's self-analysis is still necessary. Here's a case that shows why.

> *Art has done a pretty good job of preparing his insurance brokerage firm and his family for the time when he will retire as president. After meticulously updating the company's financial and strategic plans, he brought in a consultant to run a battery of executive skills tests on several family members and to match the findings objectively with the company's future management needs.*
>
> *The tests have identified Art's young nephew, the firm's hard-charging vice president for sales, as the most likely to succeed as the next CEO. The nephew knows the business, and he's an aggressive producer and a strong manager who runs his department with the latest computer programs for sales projection and prospect identification. He's bright and personable. The family would support him, and the employees would love him.*
>
> *Art is the only one who has any reservations. The nephew seems made in heaven to head the company, and he is eager to have the job. But Art just can't see placing his business, his clients, and his employees in his nephew's hands. And for the life of him, he can't figure out why.* ∎

Art is stuck with a succession solution that he can't accept, although it seems like a dream come true. His problem is not only that he put too much stock in an outside decision-making tool, but also that he didn't take the time to analyze his own role in his business and his feelings about it. He's just now beginning to realize that his personal expectations of his company's next CEO are quite different from what he's got.

Analyzing the Entrepreneur-Owner

A great deal of time and money have been spent over the past couple of decades trying to find out how entrepreneurship works and what makes successful entrepreneurs tick. Researchers, professors, and business pundits galore have conducted surveys and interviews, plotted the behavior of individuals and companies, and come up with some interesting findings. One conclusion that leaps out of all those studies is that the classic entrepreneur seems to be, by nature and disposition, the last person in the world to plan and manage family business succession.

In the first place, successful entrepreneurs tend to be very competitive and self-assured individuals who have ultimate faith in their own ideas, judgment, and capacity for hard and productive work. They are men and women who have staked their self-esteem, public reputation, and worldly goods on that faith— often more than once, because statistically the average entrepreneur has probably lost on two or three ventures before winning one. So when entrepreneurs succeed, they feel (though not always correctly) that they have done it alone, and they claim most of the guts-and-glory credit for themselves.

That heroic self-assessment can cause real problems when an entrepreneur considers the prospect of transferring the fruits of his or her success, along with the responsibility and authority to sustain them, to someone else. For example, the successful businessman loves his kids and wants all the best for them, but when the time comes to hand them the business, he may find them flatly inadequate and undeserving. In his eyes, his sons and daughters, regardless of their ages, may still look like irresponsible children, too immature to shoulder the work load and bear the strain of running the company. Or the talented businesswoman may see her family members as competitors for control of the enterprise that has shaped her very identity, pitting their naiveté, youth, and enthusiasm against her experience and advancing age. Very simply, entrepreneurs can have trouble separating their self-concept from their notions about the business. Having made their way in business by being in charge of everything, entrepreneurs equate control of their companies with control of their own lives; and giving up one means losing the other.

Entrepreneurs may also seriously doubt that their family members will ever know or understand the company well enough to run it. In some cases, that's a fair assessment. Typical entrepreneurs might be great sellers, but they are often poor personal communicators. They are garrulous promoters in public, but they resist talking privately about their company's good and bad experiences. They may not be ready, willing, or able to open up and educate their successors because they can't break the life-long habit of playing their cards close to the vest.

Finally, entrepreneurs thrive on the adrenalin rush that comes from putting deals together, leading new starts, taking big risks, winning big prizes. They are not skillful at the unexciting detail work of routine management, and winding anything down—whether it's a completed project or their role as a CEO—can bore them or scare them to death. They have achieved much in their businesses and for their families, and they are justifiably proud of those achievements. They are not at all sure that anyone else—including their own sons and daughters—could have done what they have done, and they may be right. So their view of the next generation's abilities to keep their company alive and flourishing may range from skepticism to contempt.

These same traits and perspectives can also characterize business owners who are not entrepreneur-founders. Second-generation owners of family businesses, for example, are often driven less by a commingling of their own personalities with the character of their businesses than by a need to prove that they are better CEOs than those who preceded them. If they clearly prove that point, they may have a genuine commitment to the ownership continuity of their companies as family businesses. But they may also have inherited suspicions about younger family members' capabilities, especially if they had to fight for their own parent's confidence and approval. And, research shows that second-generation owners are more likely than are founders to look for potential family successors outside the circle of their own children.

Admittedly, this picture of the successful entrepreneur approaching ownership succession is unflattering. Analyzing one's own views and values as a business owner against these benchmarks can be either exhilarating or depressing, but it can also produce some valuable insights. It begins with a review of the owner's private analysis of the company's character.

Look carefully at the lists and notes made about the company. At each point, substitute the owner for the company. For example, are the highest everyday business priorities separate from or identical to the owner's personal priorities? What level of importance does the owner attach to meeting deadlines, maintaining contacts with customers, or being viewed favorably by competitors as well as colleagues? If these things are important to the owner, is it because they benefit the business or because they make the owner feel good? How would the owner react to changes in two or three key long-standing relationships with others in the company? If a family squabble broke out over corporate policy, would the owner sit back as an aloof and pragmatic arbitrator, or would he or she feel that an attack on the company's purposes was a personal attack? What would be the owner's response to suggestions for modifying the company's character and operating style—rejection, resistance, or objective consideration?

On another level, what are the owner's deep-down feelings about the ability of someone else to run the company as well as he or she runs it? Can the owner envision being on the outside of top management decision making? What would it take for the owner to relax and trust his or her family members to set the course for the company and direct its work and its affairs? The answers to these and similar questions should reveal a lot about how personally enmeshed the current owner is with the life and character of the business. Those insights should help prepare the owner for the changes in his or her life as well as in the company's life that will result when the business is handed over to family members.

Analyzing the Owner as an Executive

The owner must now analyze himself or herself as an executive. What's distinctive about how this owner runs the business compared with the management practices of other business owners and executives? Does the owner have technical expertise that helps to keep the company on the cutting edge and to monitor the efficiency and quality of its output? How does the owner handle policy disagreements and employee disputes—by the book, by consensus, or by instinct? How does he or she approach hiring and firing? Handing out rewards and discipline?

Why does the owner do things in a certain way, and where did he or she learn to do them that way? Does the owner's way always work, or does the owner sometimes wish to do them better or differently? For example, if the company analysis showed that some form of MBWA (Management By Walking Around), as described by Thomas J. Peters and Robert Waterman in their book *In Search of Excellence*, is one of the secrets of the company's success, how vital is MBWA to the owner's sense of personal success as an executive? Does the owner's visibility and accessibility in the halls, in employees' offices, and down on the production floor actually help keep the company operating, performing, and producing? Does it give the owner a feeling of involvement and importance that sitting behind a desk does not? Is it viewed by the employees as reinforcement or surveillance? Has the company outgrown MBWA?

Finally, the analysis should pose a few questions that help focus on the current CEO's expectations of the company's next CEO. Has an executive style grown up around the company's needs, or has the company grown up around the demands of a highly individualistic style? Should a new CEO be a different kind of executive from what the current owner has been? Should the new CEO adjust his or her style to fit the company, or should the company's operations be expected to change? Are any of these points negotiable?

The analysis of the business owner and executive should offer a new view of both the intangible and tangible factors that tie the person at the top to every aspect of his or her business. These discoveries are important because a transfer of business ownership and management to other members of the family will be a lot more complicated than just passing along a warm seat in a big chair. It's something like handing down a favorite suit: the fit will have to be good, though it probably won't be perfect. A little dieting or a little tailoring may be necessary for the new owner to wear the suit comfortably without stretching it out of shape. The new owner and the clothes will have to look right together, too, because now and then the old owner is really going to miss wearing that suit.

Analyzing the Owner as a Family Leader

The juxtaposition of the owner's family and business roles, and the great possibilities and problems that it creates, may never be clearer than during the process of planning and executing the succession of ownership and management in the family business. As succession planning gets underway, it is essential to understand those roles and the relationships between an owner's responsibility to the business and duty to the family and to be prepared for the conflicts that they might produce. The following case illustrates how business and family leadership roles can interact in a succession situation.

John Wilson, Jr., thinks of himself as an open, fun-loving, and contented man. But when it comes to meeting his responsibilities to his company and to the family that it supports, he is deadly serious. At 53, John is CEO and majority stockholder of Form-Rite Concrete Products, Inc., a $30 million business. Form-Rite is owned by John, his two older cousins, and their immediate families.

John joined the company right out of college and worked his way up. When his father and uncle, founders of the business, both died within the same year, John's knowledge of the company, his management experience, and his personal dynamism made him the family's choice to head the business. He takes a great deal of personal pride in having met the family's expectations for the business's increasing profitability while keeping the company stable and rewarding for its loyal senior employees.

John has begun to think about his retirement and the options for succession in the company's ownership and management. His cousins' children are established professionals who live elsewhere. John's son Chris, who has always been close to John, will finish law school next year but has no immediate career plans. John believes that Chris could be persuaded to give up law for the family business and that he could be groomed as an effective CEO. While they want to hang on to the business, the cousins object that Chris has no relevant experience and that his liberal tendencies would soon turn the company into a socialist experiment. John pointedly reminds them that Chris will one day inherit the controlling share of the stock, although he admits to himself that right now the boy doesn't look like an ideal choice to run the company.

John and his cousins are also considering the firm's very capable and experienced senior vice president, who could do a good job as president. That choice would probably ensure the continuity of family ownership of the company. But it would open the door to nonfamily management, a step that everyone fears might eventually undermine the family's control. John must decide how to protect the interests of the business and of the family. ∎

John Wilson, Jr., successful businessman and trusted family leader, is under real pressure. His family's company is at a crossroads. His choices as the head of the business are to: (1) find and train a qualified family successor, thus keeping both ownership and management in the present hands; (2) promote the senior vice president, retaining family ownership but not management; or (3) sell the company to outsiders. He should be able to count on his proven business judgment to guide his decision.

John's choices as a family leader, however, aren't quite as clear. Always a fair man, he agrees that retaining family control of the business and its leadership is the best way to ensure everyone's future interests. While his business sense pushes him toward bringing in professional executive management when he retires, his family loyalty pulls him toward promoting his son's career interests. As CEO, John knows that selling out now at a good price would be better than letting the company's value erode under weak leadership. As a father, he secretly believes that if the family business is retained, his son can become as good a CEO as anyone and keep the control of the company in his branch of the family. He also senses that trying to push Chris down his cousins' throats could precipitate the family's first battle over the business. What kind of family person John is may determine what kind of business decisions he makes in the next few years.

Leading the Family and the Business

In analyzing the family leader who also owns a business, it's important to remember that family leadership, like corporate leadership, involves a lot more than being the biggest, loudest, strongest or oldest. A true leader envisions the future, confirms possibilities, sets goals, develops policies, makes decisions, motivates action, channels power, accepts responsibility, and evaluates achievement. A leader also sets examples, heads up parades, and is usually the first one out of the trench when there's a dirty job to be done. The congruence between the owner's executive style and family leadership style can be estimated with these questions:

■ Does the owner demonstrate the same kind of leadership among family members as among employees?

■ What leadership skills, technical abilities, and values does the owner carry over between family and business settings?

■ How and by whom are decisions made and implemented within the immediate family and among the extended family? Are the processes substantially different from those used in business decision making?

■ Is the management of the family's affairs and activities centralized in the family leader's hands, or is it delegated?

■ Does the family know the family leader as a businessperson? If so, how might that perception affect their views of and expectations of the business as a career and a major part of their adult lives?

Table 2.4 reviews these questions about the owner's leadership style.

As these and other questions about the role and style of the family leader get answered, it's important to remember that that person is usually the interface between the business and the family. How the owner plays the dual role of family leader and business executive may turn out to be the most important factor in determining if, how, and how well one or more of the family members will move into management and ownership of the company. How the owner evaluates family members' needs, capabilities, and prospects is critical to the kind of plan developed for handing over the company to them. In the same way, what the owner represents to the family about business in general and about the family business in particular is critical in shaping the family's views and choices related to succession.

TABLE 2.4 Analyzing the Owner

As Entrepreneur/ Business Owner	As Executive and Manager	As Family Leader	Needs and Expectations
Manager who keeps control Skill as personal communicator Excited by ideas, bored by maintenance Sees sons and daughters as capable adults Sees sons and daughters as competitors Closely identifies business with self	Distinctive style Essential technical expertise Where and how did owner learn to manage? "MBWA": Personal involvement in operations	Exercise family leadership? Family decision-making process Centralized management of family affairs? Family view of owner as businessperson	Should next CEO adopt current management style? Should company style change? How would owner adapt to no longer being CEO?
Bottom Line: Will the owners' commitment to your company help or hinder succession?	**Bottom Line:** How has executive behavior shaped company?	**Bottom Line:** What is the owner's family leadership role, and how does it relate to his or her business role?	**Bottom Line:** Is the owner ready, willing, and able to hand over the business?

47

The Big Question

Can This Business Be Handed Over to This Family?

There is now a composite picture that includes the business and how it functions, the family and its members' abilities and needs, and the owner as a businessperson and family leader. Some parts of the picture may be fuzzy, and some parts may seem to conflict with other parts. To answer the big question of whether the business can be handed over to the family, it may be necessary to adjust the picture's focus or reanalyze some findings and conclusions. The process must be thorough and objective. There's a big measure of subjectivity in this decision, but a gut reaction shouldn't also be a knee-jerk reaction.

In some cases, a clear answer, one that everyone can live with, will require testing by putting prospective successors into the company and seeing if they succeed. No promises should be made and enough loopholes should be left to allow the current owner and the trial successors to opt out of their arrangement as painlessly as possible.

Many sow's ears have been converted to silk purses by hard work and imagination. It may have been done when the owner started off with a run-down business and built it into a success. It could be done again by whipping prospective successors into shape as company owners and managers. If what they lack is training, training can be bought, and a lack of exposure or orientation to the industry and the business can be overcome with planning and time. But if the successor and the company do not match because of fundamental differences in goals, expectations, values, or needs, the silk purse is probably a very long shot. It's important at this point to be sure that the hopes and dreams for family business succession don't obscure its realistic chances of success. If it seems unlikely that succession is going to work, it's better not to put the whole family through the agony of proving it to the world.

If on the other hand it looks like this business can and should be handed over to the upcoming generation of this family, congratulations! But don't relax yet. The next stage in the process is developing a plan for successful succession, a plan that includes scheduling, marketing, training, delegating, monitoring, and as much concentration on the quality of effort and outcome as most business owners have put into anything they've ever done. If it works, however, its accomplishment will be as satisfying as anything most business owners have ever done.

Go for it.

Pre-Planning Analysis Checklist

This checklist is designed to help ensure that all factors affecting successful succession have been analyzed. Complete it *before* planning the actual succession.

Analysis completed?	Yes	No
1. Continuing family ownership of the business is important to:		
owner	___	___
owner's spouse/children	___	___
employees/community	___	___
2. The current and projected status of the business has been analyzed for:		
financial stability	___	___
sound strategic position	___	___
adaptability to new family management	___	___
3. The character of the company has been analyzed for:		
kind and nature of its business	___	___
what makes it work	___	___
basic and transient problems	___	___
growth history, with helps and hindrances	___	___
future goals and management needs	___	___
4. The family has been analyzed for:		
its family type	___	___
interdependent ( )		
independent ( )		
coherent ( )		
current skills and abilities of family members	___	___
direct experience	___	___
management development needs	___	___
nonbusiness needs	___	___
match of the family to the business	___	___

5. The current owner of the business has
   been analyzed for:

   feelings about the business   ____   ____

   feelings about successors   ____   ____

   executive/management style   ____   ____

   role and function as family leader   ____   ____

   expectations of the next CEO   ____   ____

6. The prospects for successfully handing   ____   ____
   over the business to the family have been
   thoroughly analyzed.

Marketing the Business to the Family

Marketing the business to the family as both a career and a family enterprise just might be the biggest and most important marketing job of any businessperson's life. In many families, it proves to be the crucial step in ownership and management succession. And, like any marketing effort, it requires fully understanding the market, assessing the appeal of the "product" to that market, and then putting together a strategy that motivates the intended customers to buy.

Why Market the Business to the Family?

Why should the business be marketed to the family? Why go to the trouble of selling the idea of continuing the family's ownership of the business? Why invest time and thought in stimulating another person's commitment to joining and carrying on a business that can provide financial support for a lifetime?

Those are good questions, the kind of questions Paul should have asked in the following case.

> *Paul's menswear store was already a family tradition by the time he took it over from his father in 1964. His grandfather had started the company more than 50 years before, and in the St. Louis suburb where they lived, the family's name was almost synonymous with better-quality men's clothing.*
>
> *So Paul had a firm, if unspoken, expectation that his oldest son James would finish college and then follow him into the business, just as he, as the oldest son, had unquestioningly followed his own father. James had had occasional part-time clerking jobs in the store during high school but had never been involved in the tedious tasks of buying, advertising, and paying the bills. Paul felt that James should have as much worry-free time as possible, because once he took over the store he'd be stuck with it for the rest of his life. Besides, Paul had learned from his father that management was a one-person job, and there would be no room for James in that end of the business until Paul retired.*
>
> *During the Christmas holidays of James's senior year of college, Paul mentioned getting things ready for his son to join the business the following summer. He had the shock of his life when James said, "Uh, Dad, I need to talk to you about that."* ▮

Paul proved to be the victim of his own assumptions. He saw himself and his son after him as links in an endless natural chain of family ownership of the store. Consciously marketing the family business as a challenging and rewarding lifetime's work never occurred to Paul (although he had sent James plenty of unconscious messages by keeping him away from the ball-and-chain of company management). James would learn what he needed to learn about the business when he came to work in the store full time, and Paul had never doubted that coming to work was exactly what James would do.

With all the built-in advantages of being the boss's kid and the CEO–heir apparent, why don't sons and daughters naturally want to follow their parents into business? Family involvement and succession are clearly factors in the business achievements of many families, and there was a time when family business continuity was a nearly universal tradition—as evidenced by such old family names as Smith, Baker and de la Forge. Before the Industrial Revolution, a son whose father was established in any line of work—whether it was shoeing horses or running the kingdom—was a lucky person indeed. Starting a business or studying for a new profession were pretty unrealistic goals for the typical young man of the time, so when he had a place at his father's elbow he jumped in and stuck with it. Of course, the tradition of taking up the family trade in those days was also reinforced by three facts of life: (1) the value of male children was widely based on their usefulness as free labor; (2) the working class lived on a pretty thin edge; and (3) not working meant not eating.

But young people today—men *and* women—have many more options and more means to exercise them. Education is almost universally available in this country. A flick of the TV remote exposes the working (though often glamorized) worlds of bankers, lawyers, veterinarians, teachers, cops. The sons and daughters of business owners are no longer obligated to follow in their parents' footsteps. In addition, parents aren't under as much social pressure to make footsteps for their offspring to follow, either. So most young people are likely to be more thoughtful about career commitments. Sometimes they are pulled away from a family business by more appealing alternatives. But other times they are actually driven away by what they see as too many negative elements in the business and in the family's relationship to it.

Long before they get to the point of thinking about the family business with any degree of seriousness, children learn a lot from observing the parent who's running it. Maybe Dad seems to work constantly and never takes time off for weekends with the family or uninterrupted vacations. He comes home glum and grumbling about his miserable day without a single enthusiastic word about its accomplishments or rewards. The business is some kind of dark force draining the family's resources, energies, and good humor. Or the business is an unknown, a black hole into which Mom disappears for hours at a time, and in front of the kids, she never talks about the business. When a person's first understanding of a business comes from evidence like this, it's no surprise if he or she later turns down the company president's job in favor of running away and joining the circus.

As they get older, business owners' children may start trying to sort through some serious questions. "What's Mom's company really like? Does she really enjoy working there? Would I?" "Would I want to have Dad as a boss or partner as well as a father? Could I hack it in business, or would I be a big disappointment to him?" "How would I ever learn enough to take over as head of the company when Uncle Bill retires?" "What's the rest of the family going to say if I don't go into the business?" If they are left to guess what the business is all about, how their parents view it, and how their own decisions would affect others as well as themselves, they may come up with a lot of wrong answers or with no answers at all.

The point is that children and other family members are always learning about the business, whether or not the owner is consciously teaching. An owner with a genuine desire to pass along the business to the next generation should develop a marketing strategy that gives potential successors a positive perspective on the company and the rewards of running it.

The Value of Marketing

Marketing is essential to the success of any business. Marketing makes the company favorably known, focuses on the interests and purchasing power of its prospective customers, sizes up its competitors, creates a demand for its products or services, and sets prices so that people can be motivated to buy and the company can make a profit. Advertising, sales, and after-sale support may be the visible components of a company's marketing effort, but they can succeed only with a coherent marketing strategy in place.

Marketing to the family is similar in several ways to marketing products and services to a customer base. Its purpose is to create a demand for the continuity of family ownership and management of the business. But at the same time it helps to create that continuity. Good marketing is a process of educating family members in the company's organization and operation. It highlights the positive features of the business without glossing over the less glamorous aspects, and it builds successors' enthusiasm for the business as a reflection of the owner's enthusiasm. It reveals the psychological and emotional, as well as the financial, benefits of life in the family business. It welcomes family members to join the business, but it never pressures or tricks them into it.

Finally, marketing helps the family and the owner to understand one another's expectations and to test their own assumptions. That's an advantage that Paul, the menswear magnate, should have seen. "I just always assumed he'd want to take over" can be a sad footnote to a lifetime's work. A carefully planned marketing approach gives everyone involved the time and the opportunity to check such assumptions before irreparable damage is done.

The Family Business Marketing Strategy

A business owner takes a big step toward ensuring the continuity of the business by beginning to work up a strategy for marketing it to the family. To the outsider, a real family business marketing process may sometimes look like a series of fortunate but unplanned events, but that's rarely the case. Developing and implementing a strategy takes work. It requires concentration on some special marketing principles. Having analyzed the business, the family, and himself or herself, the owner should be sitting on top of a pile of valuable marketing data when it's time to begin.

The five principles of marketing the business to the family are:

(1) Developing a favorable image
(2) Defining the product's appeal
(3) Sizing up the competition
(4) Pricing
(5) Selecting outlets

These principles have been adapted from standard American marketing practices; anyone who has developed a product marketing plan or studied marketing will recognize the concepts and the terminology. The applications of these principles, however, may be a little nonstandard because the goals of succession differ from other business goals.

Principle #1: Develop a Favorable Image

Prospective successors do not want to commit their working lives to businesses they know nothing—or nothing positive—about. Some entrepreneurial companies have no problem with favorable image, of course, because they have no image at all among their owners' families. Developing an image is important because people can't talk or even think very well about something they can't imagine.

When family members think about Dad's business, what comes to their minds? If they have no knowledge or understanding of the company, the only image they may get is a picture of Dad's back as he goes out the door to work every morning. Except for the kids of secret agents, that's not good. The family, especially prospective successors, should understand all of the distinct aspects of the business. These aspects need to be communicated to the family through direct exposure and a lot of discussion. The examination of the business that's done as part of the analysis for succession provides some excellent image-building material.

The business as a *place* means the actual location—the office, the plant, the store—where work is done. For some businesses, it may also mean clients' offices, airport conference rooms, hotels, and convention centers. Family members should be brought into those places and spend some time there to see how they look, feel, and smell. Someone who's being encouraged to think about coming into the dry cleaning business, for example, should know what the inside of the plant looks like. If it's a landscaping business, the person should poke around in the nursery and dig the customers' dirt. This kind of exposure is as important as hanging around the management offices, watching the secretaries, listening to the intercom buzz, waiting through phone calls, and sitting in on meetings.

The business's *environment* is also a part of its image. Environment isn't just decor or air quality. It's the physical and psychological experience of working at the business. Is there a sense of excitement? Do the employees move quickly or deliberately? Do they interact with one another or work alone most of the time? What's the customer flow like? Is the atmosphere relaxed or tense? In trying to market the business to the family, the owner naturally hopes that the business's environment looks and feels good to prospective successors.

Every business is *people*: first of all, the people who work for the business, but also those who buy its products, deliver its raw materials, and repair its equipment. The business's prospective successors should meet them and see them at work: Margaret at the switchboard, Big Jack on the drill-press, Bitsy driving the delivery van. They should learn about these people and about how their parents view them. Not every business runs as one big happy family (although research shows that family-owned businesses tend to run that way more often than do other businesses), so employees' personal lives needn't be topics for family discussion. But the people who do the company's work and make it work should be recognized as an important part of the business's image.

The family must understand the *activity* of the business. What do the people in the company do? Do they make something, sell something, broker something, service something? Do they solve customers' or clients' problems? If so, how? Every business engages in some activity that manufactures products or generates revenues. Maybe the tasks that managers and employees carry out can't be explained to the family in great detail because they're technically complex or classified, but at least outlining them is a great help in fleshing out the family's image of the business.

The business's image includes its *products*. What things or services come out of the business? Depending on their prospective successors' ages, social situations, and other factors, the book publisher, the auto parts dealer, and the condom manufacturer may have to take different approaches to building favorable family images of their businesses' products. Still, any business owner—manufacturer, wholesaler, retailer, or service provider—can be openly proud of any product that is well made and rationally priced and meets the needs of the people who buy it. Expressing that pride helps the family to develop a strongly favorable image of the business's products.

Finally, the business's image includes its net *effects*. The effects of a business's operation, products, or services—even its very existence—are felt in its marketplace and in its community, as well as in the lives of the owner and the owner's family. The effects are material, economic, and social. Some of them are easy to point out: the building contractor can point to buildings, the printer can show posters, and the advertising executive can tune in the firm's commercial spots on the kids' favorite rock station.

The car in the driveway and the college diploma on the wall are also among the tangible effects of the business on the life of the family.

Other effects are harder to demonstrate, but they include the jobs that support employees' families, the schools that are built with corporate taxes, and the ways that the business affects the family's work and recreation. There may also be some effects that potential successors view negatively: the meadow that was paved over for a new plant parking lot, for example. In mostly positive and perhaps some not so positive ways, the business is a presence, and its effects on places, people, and lives should be thought out and marketed as part of its image.

The most important ingredient in the business's favorable image among the family is the attitude of its founder or senior owner, as well as the attitudes of other family members who work for the business. The person who built the company or runs it every day should be its best representative. That person is the best source of factual information about the business—its financial, growth, and management status. Whether by choice or chance, the senior owner is also the family's barometer on the climate inside the company—how well it's going, how big the problems are, how the prospects look for next year. The owner's enthusiasm, optimism, openness, and satisfaction with the company and his or her role in it are the most persuasive factors in building the family's favorable image of the business.

Principle #2: Define the Product's Appeal

It's risky to assume that once the successors know the business, they'll love it. It's possible to create an image of the company that's so favorable it glows in the dark and still not generate much family interest in joining the business and eventually taking it over. That's why the second family business marketing principle is that the appeal of the product—*this* business—for the target consumers—*this* family—must be defined. Here's how one business owner went about it.

> *The first time Joe talked with his sons, ages 17 and 19, about coming into business with him in a few years, the younger boy asked an absolutely crucial question: "Why would we want to do that?"*

"It's a solid business," Joe answered. "It makes good money now, keeps us living pretty well, and unless I miss my guess it'll keep growing at around 20 percent a year."

"Is that good?" asked the 19-year-old.

"That's very good, compared with other businesses around here and other companies in my industry," Joe said. "It's an exciting place to work, makes top-quality products, and contributes to the community. I'm lucky to have a lot of talented people, very good people, working for me—you've met Howard, the sales manager, and most of the others. I enjoy this business more than any other work I could be doing. I think you would, too."

"Sounds great to me, Dad" said the 19-year-old.

"Yeah," his brother agreed. "Me, too. But I have a question."

"What's your question?" Joe said, priming himself to whip off production figures and sales projections.

"You wanna shoot some hoops with us or just watch this stupid game on TV?" ∎

Instead of growling about teenagers with minuscule attention spans, Joe started thinking seriously about his son's first question, "Why would we want to do that?" He hadn't really given much of an answer. He'd named the company's good points and told why he enjoyed the business, but he hadn't said anything about why it might appeal to the kids. If he was going to fire up their interest in coming to work with him and, he hoped, taking over the company some day, he'd have to spotlight the things about the business that would make sense to them.

Joe went back to the notes he'd made when he began thinking seriously about keeping his business in the family. He compared his personal analysis of the company with his analysis of the family. He'd already concluded that both sons had the basic skills and characteristics to fit into the company environment and, after getting the right training and experience, to take top executive positions—if they wanted to. He looked through his analysis of the company for features that might make them want to. When he found what he needed, he began to figure out how to focus on those points the next time he talked with his sons about the business.

What are the characteristics of a business that might turn on prospective successors and help them see the business as a desirable career option? Obviously, one asset is money. Many family businesses are able and willing to provide slightly better than competitive salaries and perks to family members who join the company. (Some family businesses adopt strict guidelines for hiring and paying family members so that this doesn't get out of hand.) There are usually better opportunities for rapid advancement and a greater degree of job security in a family-owned company, too, where nepotism is frowned on less harshly than in public corporations. And, because not all young people are the money-grubbing beasts that some surveys make them out to be, there is also the coat-of-arms factor: family ties, blood tradition, and the appeal of working with other members of the family.

The freedom and power of the private family-owned business are also appealing. Being in business for yourself is part of the American dream. The freedom to make decisions, set standards, take calculated risks, and collect rewards for success can be powerfully attractive to a young businessperson with energy and self-confidence.

Managing any company confers a substantial amount of power, and power is one of the more gratifying perquisites of authority. The sense of power in a family-owned company is often strong because it is more nearly absolute, especially when financial control is concentrated in an owner-executive's hands. While a publicly owned company may not be intrinsically more difficult to manage than a privately owned one, the CEO of an NYSE corporation lives with the spectre of hundreds of thousands of stockholders shouting in his face, "Yeah, but what have you done for me *this* quarter?" Any business-owning family that hopes to remain one will demand accountability from the person who's running the company. But prospective successors are often attracted to well-structured family businesses because their CEOs may enjoy a more clearly defined feeling of being in charge and suffer less from the unrelenting mob scrutiny that can dilute executive power in a public company.

The sense of challenge and reward is often greater in a family-owned business as well. One of the frequent (and sometimes fatal) failings of family businesses is complacency, an unwillingness to experiment and change, a lack of interest in growth. A family-owned company can be at least as dynamic and responsive to new opportunities as its more diversely owned competitors, and the point of management and ownership transition between generations is a good time to loosen things up. Offering someone the challenge of kicking the business in the pants, knocking the rust off of it, trying new things, and making rational but forward-looking changes has great marketability. The offer has to be sincere, of course, and backed up by a genuine commitment of continuing support from the retiring owner. But it can have exceptional appeal to successors and very positive results for the business.

Even the largest corporations don't waste their money by blanketing the entire American population with marketing and advertising. They target their national marketing strategies on a defined customer base, the people who are most likely to buy their products and thereby produce profits. Blue jeans designers go after the young swingers, not the serge suit types. Breweries target sports fans, not preachers. In the same way, a family business marketing strategy, beginning with the effort to build the business's image, should target those family members who are the most qualified and the most likely to join the company and become its next generation of owners and managers. If the family analysis has shown that two of the owner's kids, a niece, and a brother-in-law are the best bets to operate the company in the future, it's useless to focus a marketing strategy on Aunt Minnie (unless she owns a big block of voting shares). Image-building and the other marketing steps outlined in the following pages should be tailored to generate commitment among those family members whom the business really needs.

Principle #3: Size up the Competition

The third important principle of family business marketing is to size up the competition for the successors' future. What career alternatives, family obligations, personal interests, or other factors are competing for the commitment of the next generation? Even the person who has always wanted to come into the business is going to have to deal with pressures that may reduce his or her ability or willingness to pour the necessary energy and concentration into running it successfully. The person who hasn't accepted the idea of the family business is even more subject to the pull of competing possibilities.

Career alternatives may be the first and foremost of these. There are a lot of options out there, and some of them are going to be attractive. Corporate recruiters may offer very persuasive enticements—prestige, advancement, and starting salaries and benefits packages. The individual freedom, personal authority, and financial rewards traditionally promised by many of the professions equal those of family business, although modern physicians, lawyers, and other professionals are finding that a happy and lucrative life is no longer a matter of just hanging out a shingle.

Personal interests may also be strong competitors. The person who dreams of living in San Francisco, for example, will find it hard to accept taking over even a highly successful family business in Smallsburg. For purely nonbusiness reasons, an outdoorsy type may think backpacking for the Park Service would be more appealing than shuffling paper for the family insurance agency. Personal interests that compete with the idea of joining and taking over the family business are sometimes age-related, faddish, and transient—"But, Dad, *nobody* wants to be a sausage distributor!" Sometimes, however, they are deep-seated, complex, and quite genuine, reflecting such influences as a person's self-image, a desire to spend more time with his or her own family, or a spouse's lifestyle preferences.

Personal interests that compete with or severely complicate the prospects of family business succession shouldn't be treated lightly. More than one company has ended up closing its doors because the owner said, "Not to worry. She'll get over that 'I just don't see myself running a store' stuff."

The attraction of another career or a different lifestyle in a different place can be tough competition, yet it can be considered positive competition. *Family circumstances* can also present tough competition, which is often negative competition. The problem may be a long-standing, irrationally intense rivalry between siblings or cousins or between spouses of prospective successors. Most often, however, it is simply friction between parent and child—a clash of personalities, temperaments, or values that's so strong in some families that the younger person won't even consider working with the parent, or the parent just can't imagine the child ever becoming good enough to step into his or her shoes. Beating this competitor usually requires some monumental compromises on both sides, a settling-in period long enough to build working relationships that are viable if not downright chummy, and—if the friction has created deep resentments and mutual suspicion—help from an outside professional. When businesses and families mix, blood is not only thicker than water; it also has a much sharper cutting edge.

Principle #4: Price it Competitively

Strategic product marketing includes establishing a rational pricing structure, one that makes it both possible and attractive for the customer to buy while making it both possible and profitable for the company to stay in business. A pricing structure is also an important part of the strategy for marketing the business to the family, and it's based on three questions: (1) What are family members able and willing to pay to come into the business and take over its management and ownership? (2) What are the owner and the company able and willing to pay to have the family members do that? (3) Can all of them afford it?

The price that prospective successors have to pay to join and operate the family business may include giving up other career alternatives that are financially and personally attractive, making the natural child-to-adult transition inside the family rather than outside of it, and adjusting their expectations to meet the requirements of mixing life in the business with life in the family.

The senior member of a business-owning family, for example, can do handstands and cartwheels to persuade a son or daughter that the benefits of the family business outweigh the alternatives available elsewhere. But when the choice of a career path is made—if it's to be a satisfying choice that everyone can live with—it's the younger person who has to make it. He or she has to recognize what's to be gained and what's to be lost and has to accept the professional and personal trade-offs that go with the decision. A hundred thou' to start or the chance to run the company? A hard hat or a three-piece suit? A bucket lunch or nouvelle cuisine?

Staying close to the family in order to join the family business can also cost a young person the private molting time needed to complete the transition from dependent child to responsible adult. Under the best of circumstances, that transition is often difficult for a person to make and difficult for older family members to acknowledge. It's easier when the younger person can move out, disappear for a while, and then reappear as a new and successful individual. Part of the price that many people pay for coming into the family business is having to go through that metamorphosis in the full view, and under the judgment, of the family. That price, and the person's willingness to pay it, must be calculated. For some young people, it turns out to be a little too steep.

A related pricing factor is the adjustment in living and working conditions that a younger family member usually has to make in joining the family business. Business partners with no family ties between them can live private lives that are completely separate from their business relationship. Their families don't even have to know one another, much less eat every Thanksgiving dinner elbow to elbow.

But complete separation of business and family relationships is rarely possible when several members of a family own and operate a business together, especially in the second or third generation of family ownership. Trouble can arise from the dual relationship of the owner parent and the successor child: one is both parent and boss/partner and the other is both child and employee/partner. Giving and taking instructions, for example— a normal employer-employee interaction—generates abnormal tensions if the younger person is dedicated to proving his competence and independence as an adult and the parent is dedicated to challenging it. The situation can be even worse if one sibling supervises another. Even when a parent works hard to delegate business responsibility and keep a light hand on the controls, his or her children can feel unduly oppressed. Swallowing the resulting frustration is a price that some successors, their spouses, and their children have to pay for joining the family company. Being part of the family business inevitably means carrying over some family relationships into daily business relationships. If the family relationships themselves are stressful, that's a potential cost that must be accounted for in marketing the business to the family.

There are usually both financial and nonfinancial costs to the senior owner and the company of passing along the business to the family's younger generation, and the financial costs are easier to estimate. In marketing a product or service, of course, the company's total direct cost for making the product or providing the service, plus overhead, determines the pricing threshhold. If those costs are too high to allow a reasonable profit and continued marketing of the product, either the product or the company dies. In marketing the family business, the trick is not to allow management and ownership succession to become so costly to the owner and the company that it's just not feasible.

The financial costs of family business succession may include the actual costs of general or specialized training for successors, salaries and benefits during younger family members' apprenticeships that aren't yet offset by their full productivity, and the cost of outside consultants or other expert help that may be needed during succession planning and transition. These costs are in addition to the capital costs of any new systems, facilities, or equipment that are later proposed for carrying out the successor's vision of the company's future.

Succession costs can vary widely depending, for example, on the type of training an incoming successor needs and where it's taken or the type of consultant and his or her fee. Such costs should be estimated and realistic judgments made about their necessity and acceptability. Not all family business handovers require expensive successor preparation and special outside help in planning and managing the transition. However, where training or professional help is needed, it shouldn't be ignored because of cost. In the long run, the cost of the most thorough succession preparation the business can afford will be a bargain.

Non-dollar costs are another matter. They can be relatively minor, such as adapting the business to a new management style that both the successor and the company can live with. Or they can be major, ranging from an unplanned early retirement of the current owner to taking the company public. Some of these non-dollar costs can be controlled, and some can't. Furthermore, changes in the company's management or operating systems or in the new CEO's management style must be expected during the transition period. The president's desk that used to be kept clean and polished may get cluttered with a computer and a ten-line telephone. The company controller who embroiders every financial report with endless background detail may be replaced by a young Turk who spits out the good news and the bad news like a Gatling gun. Such changes are natural and usually necessary. In fact, a new manager who slides smoothly into the old manager's job without causing a ripple might be suspected of lacking the dynamism necessary to provide real leadership to the company. These changes and their impact on the company, the employees, and the customers should be thought out in advance and be carefully calculated as succession costs that will be billed to the owner and the business.

However, non-dollar costs of succession can sometimes be a lot stiffer. There are situations, for example, in which long-standing parent-child tensions can't be reduced enough to allow for the otherwise desirable management overlap of the older and younger generations. Where the successor is adequately prepared through training or by experience gained outside the family company, the best course may be for the older generation to step aside from active management a little earlier than planned. Sometimes continuity of family ownership and management of the business is so overwhelmingly important to the owner and the owner's family that they're willing to pay almost any price, even if part of the price is the current owner's job.

Another kind of succession cost can be incurred when founders or senior owners of family businesses decide to take their companies public for the sake of successful succession. They may choose to issue stock and sell a minority of the shares publicly in order to establish the equity value of the company for tax purposes. A public offering may be necessary to finance the growth that successors consider essential. Or the owner may find that diversifying ownership and distributing voting and nonvoting stock inside and outside the family is the best way to keep peace in the family while keeping management control where it belongs. Taking a privately owned family company public can be complicated and wrenching, especially when the company is several generations old and public ownership will bring nonfamily directors onto the board for the first time. It can also entail full financial disclosure and a new kind of management accountability. The expenses of going public—e.g., attorneys' fees, underwriters' costs, research and documentation— can be high. Going public can also be costly in non-dollar terms; if public ownership is considered as a succession option, its psychological and emotional price tag should be studied carefully.

The total costs of family ownership and management continuity should be added up and examined under a cold, bright light. Are the prospective successors able and willing to pay what it will cost them to join and take over the business? Can the company and its current family owners afford their dollar and non-dollar share of the tab? Both the up-front cost and the end price of succession should be negotiable. Maybe some new management approaches will allow the next CEO to spend fewer hours on top of the operation and a little more time with his or her family. Maybe installing an interim senior manager between the outgoing parent and the incoming child will buffer conflicts long enough to accomplish a smooth management transition.

Sometimes either the company's cost or the price to the successors, or both, may seem heavy enough to sink a family business marketing strategy and a succession plan. But because succession is a family matter as well as a business matter, owners and successors who value continuity are often willing to amortize the costs of succession—the required time, energy, good faith, and confidence in the future—if the debt service is bearable and there's a glimmer of light at the end of the tunnel.

Principle #5: Select Good Outlets

Regardless of its appeal and price, any product that isn't placed and displayed in outlets where the customer can get at it will pick up a lot of shelf dust before going back to the manufacturer's inventory. A family business marketing strategy also has to include satisfying "outlets" for everyone's ideas, interests, enthusiasm, and concerns—in the form of sound mechanisms for bringing family members into the company and transferring management and ownership. Otherwise, the strategy and any hope for the business's continuity may just languish until they're forgotten.

The next generation's entry routes into the business should be thought out carefully. How and at what level potential successors join the company may have a telling effect on how well they and the company adapt to one another. It may open up a constructive period of apprenticeship, or it may create some incorrect but terrible impressions of the business as a dreary, unrewarding grind.

The entry-level jobs proposed for successors in the marketing strategy are important first of all for the messages they send. The first real job in the family business is often seen by a young person as a measure of a parent's confidence in him or her and of his or her long-term prospects in the company. Some business owners' children grow up in the business by having small jobs— running errands, stocking, answering the phones—that are valuable as introductions to the business as a place and an environment. But when a person matures, gets a basic education, and becomes a serious senior management prospect, he or she should be brought in as a permanent employee at a more meaningful level. Executive vice president is certainly no job for any inexperienced newcomer, not even the boss's kid. But the potential successor's first full-time position should carry some real substance, or else the family business may look like an unattractive career of scut work.

On the other hand, an owner may see the negotiation of a family member's entry point into the company as a test of the person's common sense and commitment. The message "I wanna start out at the top," conveyed either directly or indirectly, can indicate that the person doesn't understand the needs of the business or his or her own readiness to meet those needs. A person's willingness to come into the company in a junior grade job where he or she can apply current abilities, learn a lot, and earn the respect of the employees can be evidence of the insight and judgment that will be ultimately needed to run the whole show.

The first job is somewhat easier to negotiate when the company has a clear promotions policy. A prospective successor can be offered a position that is consistent with his or her ability and experience, followed by advancement at the prescribed rate, though perhaps modified to accelerate progress toward the top job—if the person is good enough. A successor's accelerated advancement, however, should be based on demonstrated merit to minimize the appearance of unfairness to valued nonfamily employees.

The first job can be a little harder to negotiate when more than one family member is coming into the company at about the same time. Each person's individual professional interests and qualifications should guide decisions about his or her initial placement in the company, and a long-range plan for advancement should be worked out. After that, the person's demonstrated ability at each level of responsibility and his qualifications for the next level—in other words, the capacity to meet the needs of the business—should be set as the main criteria for advancement. Here's how that principle translated into action for one family-owned business.

Margaret had inherited a medium-size hardware store from her father. Margaret worked hard, made fair and firm deals with both vendors and customers, and built a large and profitable lumber and builders supply company. She hoped that her son and daughter would want to continue the business when she retired, so over several years she marketed it to them gently but thoroughly.

Son Bill was an easy sell. Uninterested in college, Bill came to work in the business after high school and a three-year military hitch, settling happily into a floor sales job. Daughter Betsy, one year younger, went to the state university while Bill was in the Army. In her senior year as a business major, she announced that she, too, wanted to come back to the family company and that her long-range goal was the presidency. Suddenly, Bill wasn't quite so content taking lumber orders and selling drainpipe.

Margaret sat down with Bill and Betsy and negotiated a plan that minimized sibling competition by allowing each of them to grow into increasingly responsible jobs in the company as they developed their individual abilities to meet the business's management and operational needs. Bill was offered the option of taking some time off for short-term training to upgrade his business skills, with the understanding that he would be given all the responsibility he wanted and could handle. Betsy went to work in the chief accountant's office to learn the company's financial system. Both accepted a set of objective criteria for their advancement to senior management.

Bill took a series of sales training seminars and decided that the floor manager's job, with its supervisory authority and override commissions, was his best target. He didn't complain when Betsy later moved up to vice president. After all, he was used to working for a female boss, and he liked customer contact much better than back office hassles. With a potential succession crisis under control, Margaret's only regret was that she hadn't taken the time earlier to work out a plan for her kids' placement and advancement in the company. ∎

It is important not to make pie-in-the-sky promises just to lure a son or daughter into giving up taxidermy school and joining the company. But it is equally important not to try to stick a serious successor prospect into an unchallenging, unrewarding, menial job to learn the business from the ground up. There's a lot of truth in the old saying about every journey beginning with a single step. The first step on the road to the continuity of the family business, bringing younger family members into the company, should be taken firmly and thoughtfully.

Transferring Ownership of the Business

Planning for the other aspect of the business's continuity—the actual transfer of ownership to the upcoming generation—is also a marketing activity. There are several ways to handle the hand-over of company ownership, so this is where the attorneys, accountants, and estate planners should get involved in helping to select and structure a transfer option. Each ownership transfer situation is unique and should be individually designed and managed. But here are a few common alternatives used by business-owning families.

Little by Little An approach often used by smaller and mid-sized privately held companies is the incremental transfer of ownership over a fixed period. For example, Jack's marketing strategy and succession plan might include a proposal for transferring eight percent of the wholly owned company to his sons Bob and Jack, Jr., each year for 11 years and then 12 percent in the twelfth year. The schedule is accompanied by an agreement that retains the senior owner as CEO until, say, year nine and as a consultant for the final three years. The time frame should be long enough for a smooth hand-over of authority to accompany the hand-over of ownership from one generation to the next. The family members won't have full ownership responsibility dropped on them like an anvil, Jack won't suffer the trauma of a cold turkey withdrawal from management and ownership authority, and estate taxes will be minimized. When the transition is complete, the retired owner will draw from the company's executive retirement plan, annuities, and any other special arrangements that may have been made with the family and the company.

This approach offers another practical advantage. Under the incremental transfer schedule, the family members become partners in the company, but Jack retains a controlling share of the business for the first six years. When the seventh transfer is made, however, Jack's share is cut to 44 percent, and he becomes, like Bob and Jack, Jr., a minority owner. If they were of a mind to do so, the CEO's family members together could out-vote him at that point. However, at no time can any person alone out-vote Jack and the other son. It's comforting to assume that Jack will end a career in business with a smooth, friendly transfer of ownership. But to be practical, the voting control feature of this transfer plan is also rather comforting, in case things don't turn out to be quite that smooth and friendly.

Since the incremental ownership transfer approach involves little or no financial consideration, some families have made the serious mistake of putting it into play on a handshake and a prayer. Parental trust, filial devotion, and faith in everyone's honorable intentions are substituted for a detailed written agreement, duly signed and notarized, between owner and successor. This is a bad idea for several reasons. First, both the getting and the giving up of money and power do funny things to people, including parents, children, brothers and sisters, and other relatives. Even in the best of families, people do funny things to each other in order to gain more or give up less money and power. An enforceable written contract has the effect of reducing such temptations. In the second place, having no legal documentation of a business ownership transfer can cause trouble if the company is sued or if the owner or successor dies or becomes divorced. No ownership transfer process should be started without a binding written agreement, even if the business is being given to the successors.

The Selling Alternative   Giving away a company, even to one's own flesh and blood, is not everyone's idea of a smart business move. Nor is it always a smart human dynamics move, either, because some people value a possession according to what it costs in hard dollars. So some owners sell their businesses to their successors at or below book value to ensure themselves of a predictable retirement income while letting the successors have the tax and motivational advantages of actually buying their way into the family company.

Taking the Company Public   Taking the family business public—selling a minority percentage of its stock on the open market while retaining enough ownership for management control within the family—can have persuasive appeal in marketing the business to the family. If the company is attractive to investors, an initial public stock offering can create substantial personal wealth for individual family members literally overnight. Stock in a solid company is tangible ownership, and depending on restrictions applied to the stock, successors or even former owners who become disenchanted or financially strapped always have the option of cashing out.

Going public requires opening the company to the scrutiny of innumerable lawyers, accountants, underwriters, investment analysts, and even state and federal governments. It inevitably changes the management style, accountability, and character of a family business. Despite all this, taking the company public often works as the ultimate persuader in marketing the business to the family.

Identifying the right outlets, then, is the final principle for family business marketing. Altogether, the steps in developing and carrying out a marketing strategy can provide an open, fair, and comprehensive way to integrate members of the family into the business and promote its continuity.

Marketing Tools and Approaches

Once a business owner has a marketing strategy in place, tools and approaches should be chosen that are best suited to getting the marketing message to targeted family members. There is a wide array of family business marketing tools, and many of them have been discussed earlier. Here are some of the tools and approaches that business owners have found most useful.

The Dinner Table Business Review

Too many business owners, especially some entrepreneurs, take pride in never bringing business problems home with them. Some of them accomplish this by seldom coming home. Others are simply dedicated to keeping the business away from the dinner table. But, in fact, the dinner table is where some of the most effective family business marketing can take place.

When people eat together, they are participating in a social as well as a nutritional event. Eating and talking just naturally go together. The evening meal especially is when many families catch up on one another's activities, share gossip, and make plans. Because dinner is when some of the day's best and most extended family communication takes place, it's a good time for the owner to talk family business: highlights of the day, customers and clients, funny incidents and frustrations, ideas for a new product, quick financial reports. It's also a good time for the family to ask questions and "debate" business policies. Such exchanges in the intimate, generally nonthreatening atmosphere of the family dinner table can ignite sons' and daughters' interest and lay the groundwork for a more serious introduction to the family business. In the experience of many families, the regular and relaxed dinner table business review is one of the most important tools for promoting family business continuity.

In the Office and On the Road

Most marketers try to strengthen the impact of media advertising by putting prospective customers in direct contact with their products: floor displays, test drives, free samples in the mail. The idea also applies to family business marketing. As vital as the dinner table review may be, it's still a second-hand view of the business. First-hand exposure is essential if the business is to be understood as a real thing and a real human activity, not just an abstraction described by Mom or Dad between mouthfuls of meatloaf. Letting younger family members make supervised visits to the office or the shop shows them that working in this place is okay because their parents do it. Taking older children to job sites, on out-of-town sales trips, and to trade association meetings opens up the human dimension of the business even further. There's no marketing substitute for showing prospective successors a working model of the family business.

Putting the Kids to Work

Along with seeing it, experiencing some of it, and thinking about it, prospective successors should be allowed to try their hands at doing the work of the family business. For a 10-year-old who gets to help the clerk with the light stapling or a 20-year-old who does weekly postings or customer follow-ups, active engagement in some interesting and constructive aspect of the business can be exciting. It's also not out of the question that the 30-year-old son who's opened his own engineering firm or the daughter working as a caterer can develop a positive new view of the family business if given a few consulting contracts or orders by the company. Finding real—not make-work—jobs in the business for prospective successors can be a productive marketing approach because it involves them personally and allows them to take pride in being a part of the business's activity.

The Personal Dimension

Any business runs on human energy, fueled in large part by the personal satisfaction of the people who own it, manage it, and work for it. Personal satisfaction should be a big marketing ingredient in the dinner table review, family members' visits to the office, and the jobs they do for the company. A parent's endorsement of his or her business as an enjoyable and fulfilling thing to do with one's adult life is important for the same reasons that celebrity endorsements are important in marketing products. Michael Jordan may be able to sell the kids on the virtues of hundred-dollar sneakers, but only Dad can really sell them on the personal rewards of running the family shoe store. An owner's open enthusiasm for the business—because of the independence, the power, the creative outlet, the money, or anything else—is one of the strongest encouragements for family members to become successors.

The Role of the Spouse

One of the most powerful phenomena at work in a family system is the relationship between spouses. Spouses can play significant roles in the marketing of the business to the family and in the success of the whole succession process. Even the most closedmouthed businessperson is subject to some degree to his or her spouse's influence in business matters.

> *"So, have you two been talking business again?" There was an icy edge to his daughter-in-law Wilhemina's voice when Fred and Fred, Jr., came back into the living room. But Fred barely noticed. He'd always thought that the less women knew about business the better. And besides, it was Fred, Jr., he was encouraging to come into the family business, not Wilhemina.*
>
> *For the past six months, Fred had gotten as much of Fred, Jr.'s, time as possible. He'd given the boy*

a full review of the company's structure and management and taken him to meet some of their biggest clients. The two of them had gone to a few trade conventions, too—the last one at a great resort in Hawaii. Fred, Jr., had really been impressed by what he'd seen and learned. Tonight, Fred had sketched the big picture for his son: title and compensation, stock transfer, all the possibilities and rewards in owning and operating the family company. They both felt good about the prospects.

"Dear," Wilhemina continued, "I think it's time we told your parents about our New Orleans plans." She went on at great length about how much she wanted them to move to that beautiful and romantic city, where Fred, Jr., could start his own business and she could take art courses at Tulane. "I'm sure your business—it's the paint company, isn't it?—is interesting," she said to Fred. "But there's nothing for us here. Besides, Fred, Jr., doesn't know any more about working for a paint company than I do." Fred was sure everyone in the room could hear the thud when his jaw hit him in the chest. He realized in a flash that his family business marketing plan had missed one of its essential targets—Wilhemina—and it looked like he was back at square one. ∎

Successfully marketing the business to the family—with its multiple aspects of educating, exposing, orienting, and persuading prospective successors—must reach the spouses of the family. Dinner table reviews, family councils, convention trips, and the challenges and perks of ownership should be extended to spouses as often as possible. The alternative could be the spouse's indifference, disapproval, or open hostility to a son or daughter joining and taking over the family business. In that case, there's a serious risk of having the succession plan founder or the family come apart at the seams.

The Payoffs of a Successful Marketing Strategy

To take another, but slightly different, look at some questions asked earlier in this chapter, Why all the fuss? Why is a marketing effort important for the continuity of family business ownership? What are the payoffs for the owner, the successors, and the company?

The first payoff from a sound, successfully applied marketing strategy is a better-informed family and better-prepared successors. Misunderstanding, misconception, and just plain ignorance are huge obstacles to most human enterprises and certainly to ownership continuity of the family business. What people don't know, they can't understand. And what they don't understand, they distrust or fear. The knowledge, exposure, and experience that good family business marketing gives the family in general and successor candidates in particular breaks down a lot of those barriers.

The second payoff is a clearing of the air that comes when the owner, the children, and others in the family have the chance to check out their assumptions. For example, an owner may have assumed, possibly for no reason, that his son would come into the business and his daughter would go to nursing school and marry a surgeon. The son, at the same time, may have assumed from observing Dad at the end of every day that running the company was a dull, thankless job that would make staffing a toll booth exciting by comparison. And the daughter may have assumed that she could never learn the intricacies of business management and that Daddy would be most pleased if she just stayed out of his hair.

It's only when the marketing strategy swings into gear that Dad realizes that Daughter really understands the character of the company and what it takes to sustain it. Seeing the business in depth and hearing Dad talk about what it means to him gives Son a new view of how challenging and rewarding the business could be, although he might still decide to go into banking. Daughter is surprised to learn first-hand that running the company calls for a combination of the people talents she's always had and management skills that Dad can teach her. The marketing strategy produces a complete shift of family perspective on the business and the prospects of succession. Some long-standing assumptions are confirmed, and some go out the window. But the likelihood of a family successor coming into the business and staying there is vastly improved.

Good marketing can also have a favorable impact on the other vital factor in a successful family business and a well-planned succession: the employees. As successors are introduced to the company and take on meaningful jobs that contribute to its operation, the employees start to believe that the boss is serious about preparing for continuity of family ownership. They get to know the young people who will likely be the new managers, and they get a handle on the kids' capabilities and character.

As the transition gets closer, the employees gain confidence in the owner's planning, the company's stable future, and their future with the company. Assuming that the successors turn out to bring real skills, experience, and leadership into higher-level company jobs, the employees' confidence will help to ensure a smooth management and ownership transition.

The ultimate payoff of a marketing strategy is not that it forces or cajoles kids into continuing family ownership and operation of the business. It's not that it lulls the senior owner into believing that all is right with the world and that he or she can have a relaxed retirement. The ultimate payoff is that it provides the information, experience, and perspective for everyone concerned with the future of the business—owners, successors, spouses, and other family members—to make intelligent decisions. Developing a marketing strategy often teaches a business owner some surprising new things about the business and the family. It gives prospective successors a solid basis for deciding whether or not to make a career commitment to the company, and on what terms. It helps other family members and nonfamily employees to assess the prospects for the business's stable, prosperous future in the hands of the next generation.

Informed, intelligent decision making is the fundamental feature of good management. A successful marketing strategy is worth all the time and trouble required to put it together and put it into action because it can help ensure that kind of decision making on the vital issue of family business continuity.

Family Business Marketing Strategy Checklist

This checklist is designed to help plan a strategy for marketing the business to the family, following the principles and approaches presented in Chapter 3. Check off each item as you develop a strategy specifically for your business.

	Included in Strategy	
Marketing Principles and Steps	Yes	No

Principle #1: Building the Business's Favorable Image

The business as place: family members spend time in, get familiar with places where business is done	____	____
The business as environment: family members become acquainted with the atmosphere/psychology of the business	____	____
The business as people: family members meet, learn about employees, customers, associates, others	____	____
The business as activity: family members see, learn about the work of the business	____	____
The business's products: family members learn about, appreciate products and/or services	____	____
The business's effects: family members see impact of the business on its market, its community, and the family	____	____

Principle #2: Defining the Business's Market Appeal

Marketing strategy clearly targeted to
family members best qualified to meet
company's needs   _____   _____

Specific appeals to target audience
identified and emphasized:

money/perks   _____   _____

freedom and power   _____   _____

challenge and reward   _____   _____

Principle #3: Sizing Up the Competition

Strategy takes into account competing
factors:

career alternatives   _____   _____

personal interests   _____   _____

family circumstances   _____   _____

Principle #4: Pricing Competitively

Strategy recognizes costs to family
members:

trade-offs in giving up
other career options   _____   _____

"growing up" under family's nose   _____   _____

integrating business and family life   _____   _____

Strategy recognizes costs to the owner/
company:

actual dollar costs   _____   _____

management style/personnel changes   _____   _____

owner's early retirement   _____   _____

taking company public   _____   _____

Total costs to family members and
owners calculated   _____   _____

Principle #5: Selecting Good Outlets

Family members brought on board in
meaningful jobs at appropriate levels   ____   ____

Plans/policies for successors'
advancement   ____   ____

Ownership transfer option selected   ____   ____

Selecting Marketing Tools and Approaches

Dinner table business review   ____   ____

Experience in the office/on the road   ____   ____

Putting the kids to work   ____   ____

Stressing owner's personal satisfaction   ____   ____

Marketing to spouses   ____   ____

Making the Succession Plan

Planning Early and Planning Well

The most critical factor in assuring the continuity of an entrepreneurial or family-owned business is *advance planning*. Virtually nothing except blind luck will make ownership and management succession work if no one has thought it through beforehand. For this reason, every founder or owner of a business should begin to develop a succession plan as early as is practical. If circumstances later prevent the family from continuing to own and operate the business, all that's lost is the time that went into planning. But if a CEO faces retirement—or the company faces an unanticipated loss of leadership—without a succession plan, the consequences can be more drastic. Here's an example.

> *Howard runs a custom metal-products plant in the Midwest. He makes nonstandard storm doors and windows, grain silos, and other items in one-of-a-kind*

sizes or designs. He also makes a lot of money, because his company does quality work, on time, at the right price—and it's the only one in the state. He pays himself $180,000 a year with lots of perks, and he lists his luxurious home, his garage full of Cadillacs, and a Florida condo as company property. Howard and his wife are personal guarantors on all the company's bank loans. He owns the company, and the company also owns him. Howard is 69, and after 40 years in the business, he'd like to hand over active management to someone else. His doctor has already warned him that the wear and tear of all those years and all those hamburgers on the road have put him at real risk for a heart attack.

But Howard has never given any serious thought to what might happen to his company when he got ready to step down. Oh, it's crossed his mind once or twice. Ten years ago, in fact, the attorney who revised his will pressured Howard to make some decisions about how the business would be handled when he retired. But whenever he was in a mood to think seriously about the business's continuity, something urgent always came up. Besides, thinking about retirement hasn't been a high priority for Howard, because "only old people retire."

Now Howard finds himself ready to hand over the business but without anyone to hand it over to. His older son Carl, who's 48, worked hard for Howard for a few years, and they talked of Carl one day moving up to the CEO's job. Somehow the details never got worked out, so now Carl is a manager for IBM, living happily in New England. His younger son Bruce is a local real estate agent with only minimal qualifications for running a major business. There are no senior employees ready to step into the top spot, either, because Howard's one-man management style has kept a cap on their advancement.

So at this late stage Howard faces an unpleasant fact: he has almost no options for continuing his ownership and control of his business. He could just get rid of it, of course. But the company has been the major focus of his life, and by this time his business and personal finances are tightly entangled. Selling the company would involve a lot more than just finding a buyer. It looks like Bruce or nobody—period. Howard can probably make it

*work, but it will take a few more years, and that's a pros-
pect he doesn't like.* ∎

What's the optimal time to start planning for succession in
the family business? Well, Howard, for one, will testify that it's
before the owner reaches age 69.

In fact, research on family businesses demonstrates that the
earlier the current owner begins planning for succession, the
better the chances that the process will succeed. A documentary
survey of 42 entrepreneurial and family-owned businesses
showed a clear correlation between planning lead time and continuity of family ownership. The owners of 14 of those 42 companies initiated succession planning ten years or more before
actually making the transfer of management to the upcoming
generation. Twelve of those companies, or 86 percent, made the
transition successfully.

Of the eight companies that started succession planning less
than two years before the changeover, six failed to survive for
15 more years. They either went to pieces and were sold out of
the family, or the successors let them slide into ruin through
poor management. The remaining 22 companies that began
succession planning somewhere between two and ten years prior
to transition split at about 50-50 on survival versus nonsurvival,
with the advantage going to those whose owners had started
planning the earliest.

The lesson is clear. If a business owner's goal is to hand over
the company to the next generation of the family, analysis and
planning should begin as early as practically possible.

When to Begin Planning

Some experts have pinned down the best time to begin succession
planning with amazing—even amusing—precision. One author
has suggested that planning should begin not less than 15 years
before the owner's planned retirement date. Another has ruled
that the process should start when the CEO-heir apparent among
the owner's kids is exactly eight years old. Cutting it that close,
however, is artificial and even a little silly, like buying a football
helmet for a newborn. A more realistic benchmark for beginning
serious succession planning is when it is clear that the business
is on a solid footing with strong long-term prospects, that it is
durable, and that it is something that should be kept in the

family. This approach focuses succession planning where it belongs—on the business, its management needs, and its survival. Again, however, the earlier that decision can be made and the longer the lead time that's allowed for planning and preparation, the better the chances that the family will be able, willing, and ready to take over when the time comes.

Keeping a Clear Head

To be effective, succession planning must be objective, realistic, and strategic. But it's sometimes harder than it sounds to keep all that in mind, as this case illustrates.

>   *Martha was 28 years old when her husband died in an automobile accident, and she knew next to nothing about running the paint and wallpaper store they had opened together. But with two daughters to raise she had no choice except to do her best. When customers began to seek her advice on decorating, however, Martha knew she had found a niche, and she pushed it for all it was worth—which, it turned out, was a lot.*
>
>   *Now, at age 57, Martha is exhausted. She's ready to hand over her successful interior design company to her kids and retire. Her older daughter, who's worked for her as a buyer since finishing college, will be head of the company. The daughter will get 30 percent of the business and a guaranteed starting salary of $90,000, which is 20 percent above Martha's own salary. The younger daughter has only helped out in the store periodically, but she's going to get an equal share of the business, and the company will pay her tuition at a top-flight graduate school. Martha has seen all the wallpaper sample books she ever wants to see, so she's buying a condo in Hawaii and leaving the business far behind. Her only goal is to get some rest.* ∎

After nearly 30 years of single-handedly building a business and raising a family, Martha's desire to dump it all and get away is understandable. But she's leaving a lot of loose ends behind. She's handed over a majority of her company to her children.

Only one of them will be working in it (with responsibilities she may not be able to handle and a salary the business may not be able to support), while the other one gets a free ride. Martha hasn't given any thought to her daughters' management abilities or to the long-range future of the business. She may be coming back from Hawaii before she expects to.

Planning Objectively

Admittedly, it is hard to be objective in planning for family business succession. After all, a typical owner works to maintain business continuity because of the drive to provide opportunity and security for the family and to perpetuate the company that has taken a lifetime to build. So there's a strong temptation to let judgment be overruled by feelings, to plan with the heart instead of the head.

For example, what owner wouldn't like to promise a successor a $300,000 CEO salary? It should cement the successor's commitment to the business. It would make the owner feel generous and the successor grateful, and it would tell the world that the company is a resounding success. But if $300,000 is twice what an experienced executive would be offered in the industry's open market, if the company can't afford it, if it just doesn't make good business sense—forget it!

In succession planning, there's always a danger of conflict between the values of the business system (doing work efficiently and making a profit) and the values of the family system (being faithful, even charitable, to family loyalties and perceived responsibilities). Anyone who has dreamed of seeing one of the children take over as head of the company might have imagined that child as a kind of corporate Alexander the Great: a magnificent young leader, a bold business venturer, an unerring decision maker, and someone eminently skilled in everything from financial forecasting to racquetball. It would be tempting to develop a succession plan based on that vision. But maybe the child has actually matured into a competent but fairly conservative manager, one who moves cautiously and builds consensus among subordinates instead of galvanizing them into action. An objective succession plan will capitalize on the actual strengths of the prospective new family CEO, rather than setting up unrealistic management expectations that the person is unlikely to meet.

Planning Realistically

It's also important that a succession plan is realistic, a quality that should emerge from the pre-planning analysis of the business, the family, and the owner discussed in Chapter 2. A complete and honest analysis will put some realism into (1) determining the business and family facts and characteristics that will make or break the succession process; (2) identifying the family members who possess the skills, talents, and inclinations for company management and leadership; (3) assessing the next generation's experience and needs for training for becoming effective managers and owners; and (4) devising a plan for the smooth and reassuring transfer of power, responsibility, and benefits.

Let's say that for personal reasons the owner would like to spread some ownership shares around among several family members, while keeping a majority of the voting stock in the hands of those selected to run the business. If the company's projected growth over the next ten years and beyond will provide reasonable dividends for everyone with ownership interests, then the owner will probably be remembered as a warm and generous person. But if analysis concludes that the company's future profits will not support a larger number of owners, then a succession plan that expands or diversifies family ownership is unrealistic. It will only set the stage for a family guerilla war, with periodic pitched battles and unrelenting sniping that can weaken management's operating control and drain the company of both the means and the will to survive as a family business.

Planning Strategically

There's nothing particularly mysterious about strategic succession planning. It involves setting clear goals and then laying out in detail a series of actions that must be taken to reach each goal by a specified target date. Planning a strategy for succession in the family business may be somewhat more complex than developing a five-year plan for enlarging market share, because successful succession depends so centrally on unpredictable human choices and behaviors. But the process is quite similar, and it is manageable.

Stating Goals Clearly

To develop each succession goal, the owner begins with three crucial questions: (1) What will the business need under the next generation of management? (2) How exactly can that need be met? and (3) By when? Like any short- or long-range business goals, succession goals should be hard-edged and precise. "My goal is that the company will continue to operate at a profit after I'm gone" doesn't help very much. There's no indication of what "operate at a profit" means, nor how it's to be accomplished. Also, what does "gone" mean? Retired? Dead? Moved to Palm Springs? A better goal statement would be "Following my full retirement, the company will be directed by a CEO, assisted by a three-member family executive committee," or "My daughter Jane will become chief executive officer of the company, with a 52 percent share of the ownership."

Prioritizing Goals

Succession goals should also be prioritized. An owner's natural impulse might be to ensure that his of her company's ownership and management, including the flow of ownership benefits, are controlled by designated family members. But if that goal is to have any long-term value, the business itself must survive in good financial and structural health. After all, what good will it do the family to own a worthless business? Goals for sustaining the company and ensuring the continuity of capable management should have a higher priority in succession planning than the immediate desires of individual family members.

Actions to Meet Goals

Each clearly defined succession goal should be accompanied by the sequence of actions that must be taken for that goal to be accomplished. "Form an employee council—Bob, Julia, Harry, someone from sales—to advise on management transition" might be one such action. "Bring in a management systems analysis consultant" could be another. Forget about randomly occuring events, divine intervention, and other phenomena that are beyond anyone's control. For example, "Mary marries Martin Markham, my marketing manager" is definitely not a good statement of a strategic action necessary to accomplish a succession goal. No matter how autocratic a parent may be, it's strategically unsound (and actually a bit bizarre) to put confidence in a daughter getting hitched to a rising young company star as a keystone in the continuity of the business.

Timing Is All

Good timing is another characteristic of the realistic, strategically sound succession plan. Actions and anticipated events should be put into a logical sequence that recognizes all the variables that will be in play in the succession situation. The plan should call for son Benny to head up the sales department after, not before, he's become seasoned in sales and earned his spurs. Similarly, Benny's move to CEO doesn't happen until a number of other things have taken place—not the least of which is the current CEO's decision to move over or move out. Planning for events to take place out of their logical sequence can lead to confusion, time lost to replanning, or even disaster.

The timing of succession actions should also be realistic. It's not realistic to plan for a family member who's a newcomer to the company to go from total ignorance to brilliant mastery of a complex financial structure in a year if a trained CPA couldn't be expected to do it in less than three. Nor is it realistic to expect the CEO-heir apparent to grow overnight into the shoes of a seasoned predecessor. When an energetic, can-do business owner focuses on succession planning, he or she may be tempted to get right to the goal by rushing the preparation of family members for new roles and levels of responsibility in the company. Transferring the management and ownership of a family business requires some percolation time, and cutting corners in the process is unrealistic and risky.

Who Should Be Involved in Succession Planning?

The owner-CEO is the person with the authority, influence, or control to make decisions that shape and guide the succession process, and so the burden of success rests largely on his or her shoulders. This is the person who usually gets the lion's share of the credit if the transition goes well and much of the blame if it crashes.

Going It Alone

Should an owner fly solo through the successive stages of planning and overseeing the transition to new family management and ownership? Depending on the size and complexity of the company, that may be one way of doing it. The private analyses of business, family, and self are best done as one-person tasks, with some technical help from the company controller or the accountants. In addition, some business patriarchs and matriarchs reserve all crucial succession decisions for themselves, selecting family members to join the company, promoting and demoting them at will, picking the new CEO out of the crowd of contenders, and setting down all the terms and conditions. That approach may work, but only in the presence of some big ifs: *if* both the family and the company are hierarchically structured, *if* there's a lot of raw power concentrated in the hands of the owner, and *if* the owner can plan and manage not only his or her own actions and responses but everyone else's as well.

The Role of the Board

The board of directors has a crucial role to play in succession planning. In a mid- to large-size company, the board's fiduciary responsibility to protect the financial interests of family and non-family shareholders alike is a serious matter. If board members fail to discharge this responsibility, they will be open to lawsuits by disgruntled heirs or others. The board, in turn, can protect itself with the threat of a court challenge to any succession plan that is implemented without its approval. Consulting with individual members and winning the ultimate blessing of the full board are important steps in developing the succession plan.

The directors can also help to sculpt the succession plan by advising on its various components and by managing public relations with family members and with the sectors of the community that they represent. A family-owned business of any significant size should have at least one outside director, and that person's participation and support is especially important for the nonfamily perspective and legitimacy that he or she can add to succession planning. As a group, a board that solidly backs the CEO when the succession plan is unveiled can be a great help in selling the plan to, or negotiating it with, the family. A supportive board can also be a sturdy defense against overt challenges and a calming influence on family grumbling and second-guessing.

Building Investment in the Plan

There's also a kinder, gentler—and usually more effective—approach that involves persuading family members and employees to invest personally in succession decisions. The astute succession planner applies the basic human relations technique of soliciting ideas and opinions from those who will be affected by the decisions. There are a number of constructive but noninflammatory topics for informal discussions of succession prospects: the structure of the company, its production and sales approaches, and its needs and goals for the future, to name a few.

One topic that should be avoided at this stage is individual personalities and qualifications, especially who's best qualified for what job. In the minds of most family members and many senior employees, this is the crux of the whole succession question, and they'll quite naturally be eager to influence such decisions. Accepting or even acknowledging unsolicited advice on this subject can send the wrong signals, raise expectations prematurely, and stir up dispute and disruption. The owner-CEO who is in charge of planning for continuity of the family business should never let the selection of a successor become the subject of rancorous debate.

Family and employee participation can bring useful information and new perspectives to succession planning. It has the advantage of committing people to the planning process and, if they feel that their input has been seriously considered, to the ultimate decisions, even if they don't agree with all of them. It gives family members a chance to contribute something of value to a process that's important to them, and it sustains the business as a true family affair.

On the other hand, succession planning is not the place for pure democracy in action, and it's not something that should be done by a committee. Someone has to control the flow, and that person should remember that any advice, from any source, can be either taken or left alone.

Choosing and Using Outside Help

In many respects, outside experts have the ideal job. For a limited time, they have limited involvement in a limited aspect of a company's life. They have the luxury of making recommendations and not having to stick around to implement them. And they usually get paid whether their ideas work or not.

Of course, there's a lot of tongue in the cheek of that description. Consultants and outside professional or technical specialists routinely play important roles in improving business operations by reviewing procedures, formulating standards, setting up systems, introducing new technologies and techniques, and helping to analyze and solve major problems. Consultants provide specialized expertise that a company either doesn't need or can't afford to have on board all of the time. In their best form, consultants come in, focus on the specific problem assigned to them, give advice or generate a product, and get off the payroll and out of the company's hair.

Outside resource people can play similarly important roles at various points in the process of planning for family business continuity. But their value depends on choosing and using them well. Such experts can best help in planning and managing succession not by telling the owner and the family *what* to do but by showing them *how* to do it most effectively. As preliminary decisions are made, attorneys, accountants, management consultants, and even experienced business associates can be brought in to react to ideas, interpret legal and financial implications of various succession options, or support the implementation of a succession plan. Ideally, their help should be sought when the conclusions drawn from the analysis begin to take the shape of a succession plan outline.

The Outside Attorney

An attorney with solid corporate and tax experience should be called in to review the framework of the succession plan as it relates to the company's charter, relevant federal and state laws, corporate bylaws, and other legal considerations in the ownership, management, and operation of the business. The purpose of the attorney's review is to spot any potential legal impediments to the plan and also to be sure that no options have been overlooked. The prospective division of company assets may need to be ironed out, and the relationship between the succession plan and the current owner's personal estate will require close scrutiny.

If the current owner is considering taking the company public, an experienced corporate attorney can set up contacts with underwriters and others who will analyze all the angles of a public stock offering. The attorney should also be able to advise how going public will affect the family's retention of management control, corporate and personal tax liabilities, and other aspects of the succession plan.

The attorney should produce a written report with recommendations that respond quickly but thoroughly to the owner's specific directions. As with other hired specialists—automobile mechanics to anesthesiologists—no attorney should be given carte blanche to run endlessly in whatever direction turns him or her on.

If he or she has the right credentials, the owner's business or personal attorney would be the logical choice to carry out the legal review. Perhaps good old Lawyer Bob is a longtime golfing buddy who handles wills and divorces with a real flair. But those are irrelevant considerations when the future of the family business is being laid out. If there's any doubt about Lawyer Bob's qualifications for this kind of work, a corporate tax specialist should be brought in, one who is knowledgeable about this particular industry and, ideally, who is also experienced in family business succession.

The Outside Accountant

An accountant is a useful advisor on succession planning, but he or she must be sufficiently experienced, or be backed up by a big enough firm, to examine the succession plan from the different perspectives of what's good for the business, the current owner, and the family successors. Even though they would cost less money, the company's comptroller, financial officer, or accounting staff are not the best sources of consultation on the broad range of money issues involved in succession planning. They may have in-depth knowledge of the company's financial structure and position, but they cannot be expected to overlay that knowledge objectively with the family's larger financial interests.

At the same time, the work of advising and assisting on the various financial aspects of family business succession shouldn't be farmed out in pieces to a number of CPAs. There's a lot of wisdom in the tradition of consulting with a lot of lawyers but keeping all the accounting business in one place. The accountant or accounting firm that handles the owner's personal taxes and financial evaluations may well be the best choice to advise on succession planning, since that individual or firm will know the owner's financial history, as well as the owner's financial management preferences and lifestyle. Again, however, the choice of an accountant must be based on his or her qualifications to do a large but specialized job competently. A long-standing personal or professional relationship shouldn't be the deciding factor.

From the standpoint of most owners and prospective successors, money is the most tangible component of family business succession planning. This is not to suggest that anyone's children or other relatives are crude, insensitive brutes on such subjects as family loyalty or satisfaction with one's life work. But research shows that even the desire for power and control ranks below money as the root cause of family disputes over succession. So having a solidly qualified accountant review the rudimentary plan for its financial impact on all concerned—the company, the current owner, and the successors—is of prime importance.

The Management Consultant

When planning runs into a problem that's rooted deeply in either the business or the family system, it's hard for the central players in the system—the current owner, advisors, and close family members—to analyze causes and foresee all possible effects. A specialist might bring the objectivity and expertise necessary to decipher the difficulty and suggest solutions.

Sometimes it turns out that the founder's highly individualistic management style has been a key factor in a company's past success, but that style just can't be sustained by the next CEO. Management that relies almost exclusively on the top person's vision, vigor, and instincts may be effective, even absolutely necessary, during the start-up years, but some founders hang onto that style (as a lot of entrepreneurs tend to do) while their companies mature and grow more complex. When it's time to plan for handing over the responsibility of running the business, the owner's pre-planning analysis makes it clear that the potential successors and the company have other needs, capabilities, and ideas. In such a case, solo management has outlived its usefulness and become a hazard to the company's operational health and continuity.

Rather than let this become a reason for selling or folding the company, it might be better to hire a consultant to help modify the founder's management system so that it can be directed by a capable new CEO with a different set of skills or a different temperament. A sharp consultant may look at the distribution of management tasks, where and how much decision-making authority and responsibility are delegated at various levels, reporting lines, and communication flow—maybe even the whole organizational structure. If the consultant is good, he or she can recommend ways to modify those elements logically, incrementally, and gradually, and to bring management systems into line with a new generation of realities without throwing current management, new management, or the company into shock.

The Family Business Specialist

A consultant may also be useful if succession planning gets hung up on problems within the family system. One common succession problem stems from the fact that highly competitive parents—the kind that make good entrepreneurs and successful business leaders—often produce highly competitive children. As successors, these children usually do well in the family business, too, if they and the business survive the process of getting them there.

Child psychologists point out that we learn many of our adult behaviors between the ages of five and eight. For the most part, once those behaviors are programmed in by our personal experiences and our observations of the people and the world around us, they're in to stay. So it is not surprising that a young person who grows up with an aggressive, competitive business owner as a parent proves to be aggressive and competitive when plans are made to divvy up management and ownership of the family business. Disagreements between siblings over who's being tapped for the company's top slot or whether the person getting the responsibility is also getting a fair share of the money are the causes of infighting, business and family disruptions, and lasting bitterness that ruin good companies and families every day. The chips off the old block become royal pains in the old backside, and the problems usually don't go away by themselves.

If a real family succession storm starts brewing, it's wise to put a consultant on the job before major battle lines are drawn and emotions rise uncontrollably high.

An experienced family business consultant's fee can be a good investment if an unbreakable family deadlock is threatening to scuttle the continuity of the business. While an attorney, psychiatrist, or family friend may be able to buffer warring parties, it's usually better to call in a professional or a professional team with a background in both business management and applied family dynamics—with a good measure of negotiating skill thrown in.

A qualified professional can help to sort out the basic disagreements ("I'm being asked to do the toughest job and I'm not getting either the title or the salary") from the symptomatic disagreements ("He's always been Daddy's favorite, but this is one time he won't get his way"). An outside specialist should never be used as a hired gun against the family. But if the problem is truly *in extremis*, a family business consultant may be the person with the experience and credibility to advise that succession just isn't going to work for this family and that the effort should be called off before further damage is done. Many times, however, a professional's objective perspective, fresh ideas, problem-solving tools, and ability to negotiate firmly but sympathetically can turn around a difficult situation. So a family business specialist can be very useful in unraveling family system problems and helping everyone involved to adapt constructively to realities and get focused on common business and family interests.

The Business Associate

There is also a role in succession planning for business associates who are close enough to understand the dynamics of both the family and the company and give realistic advice. Men and women who have successfully taken their own companies through ownership and management succession can be valuable resources if they are willing to talk honestly about their mistakes as well as their triumphs.

It can be both informative and heartening to talk through ideas and tactics with retired owners and with the family members who succeeded them. "Did you have a detailed succession plan in mind when your kids first joined the company? When did you start the transition?" "What more do you wish you'd known about the business before you took over? What would you do differently?" "How did you get used to not being the top decision maker? Are you satisfied today with how everything has worked out?"

Some of the answers, even from the most forthright people, should be taken with a grain of salt, because it is human nature to remember our good moves with amazing clarity while letting the dumb ones recede into the fog. Lessons that can be learned from the positive and negative experiences of other business owners and successors, however, are a real asset in succession planning. They are also less painful and less costly than many of the succession lessons that are learned first-hand.

The Employee Advisory Group

Many business owners have put together small advisory groups of longtime employees to review succession plans at more advanced stages and to orient and educate successors to company operations. The employees are usually loyal people in top and middle management and in key line units of the company. The advisory group is valuable in a number of ways. Meeting periodically during the planning and transition stages, the group forms a pipeline linking current and new management with the company's employees. It helps to keep selected information about succession plans flowing to the general employees and to communicate the employees' reactions back to management. Because the lack of basic information about succession-related changes and their impact on policies, operations, and individual employees is a major cause of organizational stress, the advisory group can be a source of reassurance and support.

An employee advisory group also can bring a very practical perspective to succession planning. Since it is inevitable that new family management will make some changes, the advisory group can help to pinpoint operational areas where changes would be constructive. The advisory group can react to prospective new policies or management and ownership structures that will affect employees directly, helping to head off morale and productivity problems that might result from well-intentioned but poorly informed new directions from the top.

An employee advisory group formed during the succession planning process may be kept intact to help smooth the management transition by bringing the new CEO, other managers, and other family members up to speed on how the business really works at the nitty-gritty level: the quirks and preferences of important customers, the best and worst days for moving paperwork through accounting, little flaws that might cause big trouble with the shop safety inspectors, the real reasons why inventory is always underreported. The old military saying "All the brains ain't in the officer corps" has a lot of meaning in a business setting, too. Of course, most companies wouldn't run very well if every management question were put to an employee vote. So the advisory group's role in succession planning should remain advisory and not be allowed to become legislative.

There are valuable roles to be played in the succession planning process by professionals and nonprofessionals, people inside and outside the company, and the family. Here's a word to the wise, however. Family business combines two subjects of universal interest to human beings—someone else's family and someone else's business. Outsiders sometimes push hard to get closer to the decision-making center of things than they need to be. This may be less the case with attorneys, accountants, and other professionals than it is for business associates, friends, employees and others. When the planning gets complicated or the transition gets rough, it is tempting to confide in anyone with a sympathetic ear. But it's a bad idea to give too much information or too big a vote to people who will not have to live with the consequences. Keeping family business decisions as the property of the family is worth risking the alienation of a few well-intentioned outsiders.

The Well-Turned Succession Plan

There is no standard, one-size-fits-all family business succession plan. Both families and businesses come in an infinite variety of shapes and configurations, and each one has its own set of potentials, problems, needs, and characteristics. Each family business must have a plan for ownership and management succession that is conceptualized, structured, and timed to fit that family and that business. But there are some guidelines, based on research and tested by the practical experience of business-owning families, that can help in developing an individual family's succession plan.

The succession planning organizer at the end of this chapter shows what to include, and in what order, in a comprehensive plan. The organizer is more than an outline and less than a sheet with a few blanks to be filled in, like the "incorporate yourself" forms advertised in airline magazines. As a guide to building a succession plan, the organizer incorporates information on the business and the family, the goals of the succession plan and the steps required to reach them, statements of roles to be played by key people in the process, and an estimate of the dollar costs of succession. When complete, the organizer should suggest a basic plan that provides a solid but flexible platform for managing the transition of family business management and ownership.

The completed succession plan should clearly describe the family's succession process and the actions that should be taken to ensure successful succession. It should work like an operations manual, with the important goals stated in priority and the steps set down in their logical sequence. It should be used as a kind of textbook to help educate family members, both those who come into the business and those who don't. It should serve as a reference for the owner and other family members to turn to as the transition process goes forward and when it is successfully finished.

What the succession plan should not do, however, is work like the Ten Commandments. All succession plans have to be fleshed out and modified, perhaps many times, as they're being carried out. People change their minds, events take unforeseen turns, accidents happen. The business owner who plans and manages the transfer of a business to family members must be prepared for a few detours from the charted course. But at least there will be a charted course, and that will be a lot better than wandering aimlessly from one frustration to another.

The succession planning organizer may look like a bear to complete. In one respect, that's exactly what it is. But completing it will give owners and their families a firm grasp of the steps required to plan and execute business ownership and management succession. It will also provide a working tool for managing the transition process.

The Succession Planning Organizer

For this organizer to be of value in building a family business succession plan, all sections of it must be completed *in writing*. All information, facts, and opinions must be accurate, honest, current, and complete.

I. *A Description of the Business*
   1. Legal description
      a. Charter: Sole proprietorship ( ) Partnership ( )
         Closely held corporation ( ) Public corporation ( )
         Founded in 19 _____ Founded by _____
      b. Current owners and investors:
         Name: _____ Ownership: _____%
         Name: _____ Ownership: _____%
         Name: _____ Ownership: _____%
         Name: _____ Ownership: _____%
         (Continue on separate sheet if necessary)

         Officers by name: _____ President
                           _____ Vice-President
                           _____ Secretary
                           _____ Treasurer
         Directors: _____
                           _____
                           _____

   2. Strategic description
      a. Nature of the business: What is this company in
         business to do? _____
         _____

         What are all of its revenue-producing activities?
         (1) _____
         (2) _____
         (3) _____
         (4) _____
         (Continue on separate sheet if necessary)

b. Market position: By market share or rank (e.g., first, second, tenth), what is the company's position in its market? _____

c. Reasons for success: What are the three things most responsible for its current level of success?
   (1) _____
   (2) _____
   (3) _____

d. Strategic goals: What are the company's three most important goals for the immediate and long-term future?
   (1) _____
   (2) _____
   (3) _____

3. Organizational description
   a. Organizational chart: What are the lines of supervision in the company? Does the business have an up-to-date organizational chart? (If not, draw one.)

   b. Working organization: Briefly describe the key jobs and duties of the owner(s), managers, and other employees in the company.
   Owner(s): _____
   _____

   Other executive(s): _____
   _____
   _____

   Manager #1: _____
   _____

   Manager #2: _____
   _____

   Other key employees (by name or job): _____
   _____
   _____
   _____

II. *A Description of the Family*
   1. Family boundaries: What persons are included in "the family" for purposes of planning business ownership succession?

_____   _____
_____   _____
_____   _____

Who in the upcoming generation is likely to inherit or
otherwise receive ownership?

_____   _____
_____   _____

What change will that make in the current
distribution of ownership and control of the business?

_____

2. Family members in the business: What relatives are
   now involved in the business as owners and/or
   employees, and what are their jobs or other roles?

   Name   Role

_____   _____
_____   _____
_____   _____

(Continue on separate sheet if necessary)

3. Successor qualifications: Which members of the family
   are qualified by training, experience, and/or interest
   for management positions in the company? According
   to the best evidence available *at this time*, for what
   job is each person best suited? What additional
   training or experience would each person need in
   order to become fully qualified for that job in the next
   generation of company management?

   | | Possible Future | Training/Experience |
Name	Position	Needed
_____	_____	_____
_____	_____	_____
_____	_____	_____

4. Family needs: What family needs—financial, career,
   other—will the business be expected to meet over the
   next 10–20 years? (Be as specific as possible.)

_____
_____
_____

III. *Overall Goal of the Succession Plan*
In clear and direct terms, describe the result that should be produced by this succession plan if it is completely successful. In other words, what should be the specific role of the family in the business, and what benefits should the business be providing to the family, 20 years from now?

_____
_____
_____

IV. *Specific Succession Goals and Actions*
List a minimum of five specific succession goals that must be achieved if the overall goal is to be achieved over the next 20 years. List these goals in a logical sequence (i.e., order of importance or chronological order), remembering that sustaining the business should be of greater *immediate* importance than meeting family members' needs and desires.

Under each goal, list the sequence of actions, in chronological order, that must be taken to achieve that goal. Give a target date for each action. (Continue listings of goals and actions on separate sheet if necessary)

Goal #1: The first goal is to: _____
_____

First action: _____
_____ Target date: _____
Second action: _____
_____ Target date: _____
Third action: _____
_____ Target date: _____

Goal #2: The second goal is to: _____
_____

First action: _____
_____ Target date: _____
Second action: _____
_____ Target date: _____
Third action: _____
_____ Target date: _____

Goal #3: The third goal is to: _____

_____

First action: _____

_____ Target date: _____

Second action: _____

_____ Target date: _____

Third action: _____

_____ Target date: _____

Goal #4: The fourth goal is to: _____

_____

First action: _____

_____ Target date: _____

Second action: _____

_____ Target date: _____

Third action: _____

_____ Target date: _____

Goal #5: The fifth goal is to: _____

_____

First action: _____

_____ Target date: _____

Second action: _____

_____ Target date: _____

Third action: _____

_____ Target date: _____

V. *Succession Roles and Responsibilities*
    List the individuals—current owner(s), owner's spouse,
    owner's children, other relatives, attorneys, accountants,
    consultants, company employees, and others—who will
    play key roles in carrying out this succession plan.
    Describe the responsibilities that each person should take.

Name	Responsibilities in Plan
_____	_____
_____	_____
_____	_____
_____	_____

(Continue on separate sheet)

VI. *Costs of Succession*

    1. Succession training: Estimate the cost of $_____ education and training that individual family members may require for succession purposes.

    2. Outside help: Estimate the cost of $_____ consultants and other specialists whose help may be required during the transition process.

    3. Successors' salaries: Estimate the cost of $_____ salaries and benefits that will be paid to successors during their apprenticeship(s). Note if these salaries will be greater or lesser than salaries and benefits payable to nonfamily employees in the same jobs.

Total Estimated Cost
of Succession $_____

C h a p t e r 5

Being
Businesslike

Some tough decisions have to be made in planning and managing
succession, and they're made tougher by the knowledge that the
company's future and possibly even the family's future may be
riding on them. Chapter 2 discussed the importance of analyzing
the carryovers between leading the company and leading the
family. Sometimes it can be important to keep those roles separate, because there are occasions during the transition of business ownership and management when the senior owner—and
the upcoming generation, too—must suspend family ties and be
thoroughly businesslike in making critical decisions, in giving
direct and unpleasant instructions, and in saying "Absolutely
not!" when it's necessary.

Succession Management
Touchstones

Family business research and the practical experiences of business-owning families have generated a set of useful guidelines

for making transition decisions, acting on them, and evaluating their impact. These touchstones are helpful in maintaining a businesslike manner throughout the transition, and they can provide reference points during those inevitable times when the going gets tough. Remember to adapt them to the circumstances and personalities of individual situations.

Stone #1: Preserve the Business

In order to hand over a business successfully, there must be a business to hand over. Exercising sound judgment to preserve the business during the excitement or urgency of management and ownership changeover can be harder than it sounds. But it's essential that choices and decisions be made with an unwavering commitment to protecting the business.

Succession actions are not in the company's best interest when they put control in the hands of uninterested owners or weak executives, vastly overextend the credit line, drain the company of cash, undermine solid relationships between managers and employees or among employees, or make customers and suppliers nervous. Nor are such actions in the best interests of the family or of business continuity. At every step of the succession process, the business's needs must be considered before the family's immediate wishes. Otherwise, there might not be enough of the business left at the end of the process to justify the effort.

Stone #2: Run It By the Numbers

Managing by the numbers—making decisions on the basis of cost and price, profit and loss, track records, and projections—is a sure (although some would say unimaginative) way to keep a company on an even keel. "By the numbers" can also describe a businesslike approach to decision-making in managing succession. It implies keeping the decision making process clean, free of the clutter of improbable hopes and unwarranted assumptions, and focused on the objectives of the succession plan. People's feelings are involved in family business succession, and those feelings should be respected as much as possible. But at the same time, feelings shouldn't be allowed to muddy up the planning, preparing, and managing of succession.

Stone #3: Don't Duck the Tough Decisions

Owners and CEOs of companies must deal with both the blessings and the burdens that come with top decision-making authority. That authority, and the satisfaction it produces, is one of the blessings of business ownership. It can be a burden, though, when a decision is particularly crucial and, at the same time, difficult to get a handle on. The good manager collects all the facts, thinks through each option and its consequences, and then proceeds to make a decision and act on it. Managing the hand-over of the family business brings up a lot of tough decisions, and it's a temptation sometimes just to ignore them and hope they'll go away. They won't. To paraphrase one of Murphy's laws, any difficult succession situation, when left alone, will inevitably get worse. When there's a decision to be made, the best and usually least painful approach is to make it as intelligently as possible and get on with the job.

Stone #4: Plan and Manage Strategically

Strategic planning and management basically means planning for and acting on events and actions over the long term. In managing ownership succession, it means having a plan for the whole succession process, either from beginning to end or from major event to major event. It also means dealing with the changes in the company's business environment that will occur during the transition period and the changes in personnel, procedures, and policies that will be produced by a management-ownership transition. Planning strategically also includes preparing for succession-related expansions and constrictions in the company's operations, products, and finances. Engineers don't put up a highway bridge by starting at one side of the river and building straight across. They build strategically, drafting blueprints, measuring the water depth and currents, calculating stresses and loads, starting at both ends, and working toward the middle. Business owners and their families should also plan and manage strategically in bridging the generations of business ownership.

Stone #5: Know and Obey the Law

Some business owners and their heirs go right to—or beyond—the limits of legality when transferring assets in an attempt to either avoid taxes or fool creditors. Sometimes it's because the business is dancing on a financial tightrope. Other times, it's just for the sheer delight of pulling off something slick. In either case, the dollars saved in the short term aren't worth the risk of having the business bushwhacked by the IRS or the bankers just when the next generation of management is trying to get its feet on the ground. It's smarter to consult the lawyers and accountants on what's legal and what's not. Then, go with what's legal.

Stone #6: Neglect No Detail

Managing family business succession is a little like starting a new business. Most people only do it once. It requires a lot of planning and work. It can sometimes be frustrating and scary in its early stages and is usually immensely satisfying when it succeeds. And it involves innumerable details. Management of the succession process demands that every detail be anticipated, attended to, and accounted for. As Joseph Mancuso says about starting up a company, the person in charge doesn't have to handle every detail perfectly, but he or she has to handle every detail somehow.

Stone #7: Stick With the Program

In managing ownership transfer to the next family generation, business owners are sometimes tempted to start making it up as they go along. This is especially true when the business is relatively small and the process seems to be going well: everyone is coming on board as scheduled, the employees and the family are happy with the prospects, and the business is flourishing. The hand-over seems to be going flawlessly, so why not embellish it by adding a couple of new directors or organizing an employee stock ownership plan right on top of everything else? But a succession plan that has been established, accepted, and implemented shouldn't be tinkered with except for very good reasons. Impulsive changes in plans and shortcuts in managing the transition can create unnecessary and unacceptable risks.

Stone #8: Trust Your Business Sense and Intuition

The man or woman who has built a successful company and managed it effectively through the ups and downs that every business endures has usually developed a reserve of sound business sense and intuition. If that small voice starts to whisper that something's not right about the transition, it should be listened to. Often, the subtle things, the things that can only be detected by a well-tuned business intuition, either make or break succession.

Stone #9: Keep a Firm Hand on the Throttle

Growing too fast is a life-threatening hazard for any company, and moving too fast in the ownership transition process can be life-threatening to a family business. While moving too slowly might frustrate the upcoming owners and managers, racing through the process can put too much responsibility on the shoulders of half-prepared family members, throw employees and customers into shock, and shake up the operating rhythm of the whole company. The sequence and timing of events and actions worked out in the succession plan should be followed carefully. The speed of the transition should be kept under control.

Stone #10: Keep an Eye on the Break-Even Point

A new company reaches its break-even point when revenue equals cost. There's no profit yet, but the income and the outgo are in balance, and the color of the ledger ink switches from red to black. In the process of handing over business ownership and management, the break-even point is reached when the senior generation and the upcoming generation are full partners in running the business. All of the actors are doing their jobs well and pulling their share of the load responsibly. The transition process feels right, and that usually means that it is on track. Of course, sensible managers do not settle for just maintaining a break-even status; they are in business to make a profit, and so they push on toward that goal. Business owners who are committed to continuity of their businesses will not settle for only maintaining a partnership with their successors, either, because their goal is to hand over the company's full management responsibility and ownership. But the break-even point is an important milestone in managing succession. It's an indicator that success is within reach, and it's important to recognize it when it comes.

These ten touchstones (summarized in Table 5.1) are helpful in maintaining a businesslike approach to decision making in

TABLE 5.1 Succession Management Touchstones

#1 Preserve the Business	#6 Neglect No Detail
#2 Run It by the Numbers	#7 Stick With the Program
#3 Don't Duck the Tough Decisions	#8 Trust Your Business Sense and Intuition
#4 Plan and Manage Strategically	
#5 Know and Obey the Law	#9 Keep a Firm Hand on the Throttle
	#10 Keep an Eye on the Break-Even Point

managing succession. What follows is a look at some of the major decisions that have to be made during the transition.

Somebody has to Be the Boss

The toughest and most sensitive decision of all is usually the choice of which family members are going to run the company. The choices that are made, as well as how they are made and acted on, will have a big impact on the future of the company and the family. But the good news is that after the executive issues are dealt with, a lot of other things will fall more naturally into place. Here's how it worked for one business owner.

> *Stan had a small but very profitable medical equipment company. He had three kids. He also had a problem. His plan to pass along ownership of his business hit a snag when it came time to choose which person would be named head of the company. But Stan's problem wasn't that none of the kids was qualified to run the business. His problem was that they all were!*
>
> *His oldest son, Bob, had gotten an M.D. degree but had gone to work in pharmaceutical sales instead of going into medical practice. When Bob came to work for Stan, he turned out to be a solid and experienced sales leader, and the M.D. on the end of his signature carried a lot of weight with customers. Catherine, Stan's second*

child, had joined the company right out of business school and was a no-nonsense star in the finance department. Danny, the youngest, was hard-driving, ambitious, and a genius in marketing; he'd worked for another company in the industry for three years but was now ready to settle into the family business.

Stan's analysis of the company's long-term management needs and each person's ability to meet them had turned up a three-way tie. Over the years he had given each person opportunities to grow in the business without grooming any one of them as the next boss, and they had all made excellent contributions to the company's operation and growth. But a choice had to be made, and it couldn't wait much longer if Stan was going to keep to his schedule for handing over the top management and retiring.

Stan's management experience told him that good decisions aren't made in a closet. So he organized Bob, Catherine, Danny, and himself as a strategic analysis team. Swearing themselves to objectivity, they met regularly for eight months to sort through the alternative directions the company could take over the next 20 years. They analyzed the impact of having the firm headed by each person: a sales expert, a financial manager, or a marketer. In each case, they also designed very specific procedures to ensure that the other siblings, and the expertise they represented, could have direct inputs into top management decision making. With the help of a couple of consultants, the team examined possibilities for a new leadership structure and equitable compensation.

At the end of the eight months, Stan's succession problem was solved. The strategic analysis team concluded that the company's best future prospects lay with Catherine as CEO and Bob and Danny as senior vice presidents. They put together a succession plan to avoid future problems if for any reason Catherine had to be replaced before she retired. The exercise also welded Stan's three kids into a solid management decision-making team. Stan looked forward to retirement with real satisfaction and confidence. ∎

Stan's plan was a winner, in part because Bob, Catherine, and Danny were each able to be objective and to realize that if the company thrived, they all thrived. Not all business owners are that fortunate—or that smart. Many who seem to believe in inherited executive prowess fall back on what a *Wall Street Journal* article called the "lucky sperm" rule for selecting the next company president: the person who is lucky enough to have been born first, regardless of qualifications, gets the job. (Some make a bad idea even worse by adding a "lucky chromosome" provision so that the new CEO has got to be not only the first-born but also the first-born male.) The business owner who goes with the lucky sperm rule may think that the choice of successor was made in heaven. But the anger and dissention that this irrational approach can stir up in the family will make the idea seem like it came from some entirely different place.

The experiences of many business-owning families show that the best approaches to choosing the next CEO are based on the suitability of the individual candidate for the job. If Number One Son has technical training, proven management skills, and on-the-job experience, he ought to get the nod—if heading the company requires a lot of technical activity, quality control, and working on the line to crank out the product. But if Number Two Daughter, or even Number Five Nephew, demonstrates a superior planning and decision-making capacity and has the full confidence of employees, directors, and customers, that person might be a better bet—if that's the nature of the company and the CEO's responsibilities.

It's more reasonable to choose a successor who fits the job than to choose a successor and then try to make the job fit the successor. No one should be chosen on account of family-designed genes or simply because he or she is available when a choice has to be made. It's better to turn to a professional manager from outside the family than to choose a CEO based on weak, unbusinesslike criteria.

Using the Planning Analysis

Making choices for the top jobs in the family-owned business is a lot easier if a thorough analysis of the business and the family has been done very early in the succession planning process. A good analysis, as outlined in Chapter 2, not only spotlights individual family members' skills and abilities but also helps to create an understanding of how each family member would function in the total context of the company.

Management selections are even more businesslike and more durable when they're also based on a hard-nosed assessment of each candidate's preparation, job performance, and other demonstrated executive qualifications. Family business questions are always influenced to some degree by personal considerations. But choices of the next occupants of the company's highest chairs should be made objectively and with the interests of the business in view.

The Price of Waffling

Without being carelessly hasty, decisions on the next generation of company leadership should be made and announced as early as possible in the transition process. There's little to be gained and much to be lost by waffling on that crucial choice or by keeping the choice secret.

"Waffling" is defined by Webster's as equivocation or reluctance to commit oneself to a position or an interpretation. In managing family business succession, waffling on naming the next CEO and other senior executives is like being a little pregnant: it creates a condition that just grows and grows in magnitude and complexity. Extended waffling, even with the best of intentions, produces a corrosive situation. Let's say it's an established fact that the senior owner is going to retire and hand over the running of the business to someone in the family. The management and ownership transition is underway, but the senior owner can't bear to hurt anybody's feelings by coming right out with a decision that elevates one family member over the others.

No one wants to seem too grabby by pushing openly for the top job. The owner's spouse may not want to play favorites or may just want to stay out of the whole thing. If the family isn't used to sitting down together and discussing problems openly and directly, there's no forum for airing good ideas and ventilating the bad feelings that inevitably build up as the decision is delayed.

And so it goes. Everybody is waiting for a decision, and nobody is making one—or at least not announcing it if the decision has been made. Nerves become frayed. Spouses get tense about the future. Employees start watching the calendar. Morale sinks in the office and at home, productivity falls off, and family members start plotting ways to force a decision in their favor.

Things may finally reach the point of a blow-up, complete with hysterical judgments, shouted accusations, some people leaving the business and the family altogether, and wounds that don't ever heal—the very thing that everyone wanted to avoid.

Choosing a person to take over as head of the family company and announcing that choice as soon as it is made creates several positive effects: First, it gives the CEO-designate valuable time to concentrate on preparing for new duties and for developing a new leadership perspective on the company and the family. There are some profound psychological and practical differences between being the boss's kid, bubbling with new ideas about how the company ought to be run, and actually being in charge and responsible for running the company. The adjustment takes time, and the new CEO must have the chance to get up to full speed before the baton is passed.

Second, making the decision and the announcement early gives everyone else time to adjust to the new structure. When a family-owned business names a new chief, a number of business and family roles and relationships shift. Other family members and employees need to sort out their places in the new arrangement, even if it's not going to take full effect for several years. Some people may start lobbying quietly for better jobs under the new executive. Others may decide to leave. Having additional time to compensate for such secondary changes in the company and the family is vital to a nondisruptive handover of authority when it comes.

Finally, early identification of the new leadership helps to prevent a crisis of confidence in the company. Planning ahead for the continuity of the family business scares some people because it confirms that the senior owner is not, after all, going to be sitting behind that big desk forever. An unknown change is coming. As that fact sinks in, employees, stockholders, bankers, and others with a stake in the company's long-term future start looking around for the new pillar that will hold up the business. They don't necessarily lose respect for the current CEO's leadership, but at the same time they want to be assured that although the person at the top will change, the company will go on as always.

A major public corporation usually announces its CEO's retirement and the appointment of a replacement at the same press conference in order to minimize the uncertainty caused by a leadership change. Perhaps on a different scale, but for the same very good reason—sustaining confidence and loyalty in the company—a change at the top of a family-owned business should be decided and announced early in the transition process.

Is it Possible to Satisfy Everyone?

It would be comforting to think that an early choice and announcement of the next head of the family company would keep everyone calm and happy. That's often the case, but not always. If the people who don't get top jobs feel that they've been ignored, or if other family members or employees think their interests have been overlooked, there will be some disappointed, hurt, and angry people storming around. There may, however, be ways to avoid or minimize such problems.

In *Motivation and Personality*, psychologist Abraham Maslow observed that all people generally share the same basic desires. The forms that those desires take—a new car, a new house, or the presidency of the family company, for example—are means, not ends. In other words, all human beings have only a few fundamental goals, and each individual desires things that he or she perceives as significant mileposts along the road to achieving those goals.

The differences among us, says Maslow, are in the ways we express and satisfy our desires. Person A's desire for the presidency of the family company may actually be a desire for power and authority over the lives and actions of others. At the same time, Person B's desire for the same presidency may reflect an underlying desire for greater recognition of professional abilities and his or her value to the company and the family. It's possible to satisfy both people with decisions that give the presidency to only one of them but that help both of them to fulfill basic desires. The trick, of course, is uncovering the real desire that each is expressing in terms of the presidency.

Amateur psychoanalysis is always risky because it can create more problems than it solves. But there are some other sources of insight that can be useful in making decisions on the next generation of family business leadership. The view of the family that emerged earlier in the pre-planning analysis may have produced some useful information on the orientation, ambitions, and quirks of family members.

For example, if the family analysis shows that one person's principal interest, training, and orientation are in the business's technical side, that person may want to be CEO in order to get the authority to install state-of-the-art innovations and propel the company onto the industry's technical cutting edge. Another person who needs a substantial flow of cash and who feels a strong commitment to his or her own family may see the presidency as the means to a better salary and to improve his or her children's future ownership positions in the family business.

In managing the transition process, it's important to remain objective in sorting out and dealing with these desires, just as it's good negotiating technique to learn what motivates each player. The most constructive position is that there is nothing inherently better or worse about either person's ambition; they are just different desires expressed in the same statement: "I want to be the next boss!"

It might be possible to satisfy the first person by restructuring management to include a vice president for research and development who has considerable authority to put new technical standards and operations in place in the company. The other person's desire for financial security could be met by a thoughtful plan for distributing ownership benefits among all the family members—taking care, of course, not to hobble the company financially.

Is it possible to satisfy everyone? Never completely, of course. But in the succession situation, some strategic moves can help to meet family members' basic desires while separating those desires from the issue of who's going to be the next CEO. If the moves work, there's more decision-making flexibility for the senior owner and a more supportive family atmosphere during the management and ownership transition.

Planning Fair Financial Incentives and Provisions

A lot of jokes have been made about the loser who sniffs indignantly, "It's not the money, it's the principle of the thing." In many family business succession situations, the principle of the thing may be at the core of people's desires and their satisfaction or dissatisfaction with how those desires are met. Still, money is very important, and managing succession in a businesslike way must include making fair provisions for the financial positions of the family, the employees, and the company. At this point, it's essential to call in outside help from tax, legal, and estate planning experts.

The Family Inside the Business

The point was made in Chapter 1 that there's a big difference between owning a company and running one. The dollar dimension to that difference makes it advisable in succession planning to sort out salary and benefits from compensation and both of them from return on equity.

Let's say that Nephew Nyles comes to work for the company as a sales representative. Although some might think he owes the company something because it's a family business, Nyles doesn't come in like an oarsman in a slave galley. He signs on for exactly what every other sales representative is getting: a competitive base salary, probably supplemented by some formula for crediting his sales commissions, and a standard schedule of benefits. Nyles spends his days on the phone, on the street, in the customer's shop, moving the products. He turns in his orders and expenses and picks up his check. At the end of the year, he may get a bonus based on how well he did against his sales targets. The fact that he is the owner's nephew has no effect on how or how much he is paid for working for the company— because Nyles has *no more and no less responsibility to the family business* and to the family than any other sales representative has.

After a few years, Nyles's productivity and management ability earn him the job of vice president for sales. This is an executive position, and it brings Nyles more headaches but also a richer compensation package. In addition to a higher salary and fatter bonuses based on the productivity of his entire division, he also might get stock options, a big car, and a much better retirement plan. These perks and incentives are no more and no less than the industry standard. At this point, Nyles has more responsibility to the company than do others in the sales force, but he has *no extraordinary responsibility* to the family. Nephew or not, he's still in the category of hired help.

Then the senior owner retires after putting together a succession plan that makes Nyles president of the company. Nyles has just become responsible both to the company, as chief executive, and to the family for setting strategic directions that will ensure the company's continued growth and success and the continuity of the family's business heritage. Nyles shares majority ownership of the business with a couple of cousins who are also company executives and directors. The succession plan gives him a president's salary, bonuses, and perks, along with a nice chunk of equity in the company. He shares in the company profits that he's responsible for generating. He earns his share not by being Nephew Nyles but by producing measurable results against a realistic standard, and by *providing overall leadership to the business* that produces income for the family.

The point is that younger people who work for family businesses should be compensated at the level of their market value to the business until they rise to management and leadership positions where their larger responsibility to the family kicks in. Even then, their compensation should be objectively indexed to their performance against targets that have been set and mutually accepted in advance.

Gloria Ewing is a compensation specialist with the Chicago accounting firm of Blackman Kallick. She encourages family-owned businesses to structure compensation for rising young family executives according to the company's strategic plan and a concrete performance measurement system. One of her specific recommendations is that compensation include a discretionary salary plus a specified share of total profits based on performance. If a family executive wants more money out of the business, he or she gets it only by producing more revenues and enhancing profits.

This approach, says Ms. Ewing, is simple, reasonable, and equitable in most family business settings. It tends to eliminate a lot of the common grounds for financial squabbling during the transition. And it ties family members' compensation and equity earnings directly to their responsibility for the overall profitability and welfare of the company.

The Family Outside the Business

Dividing the family business's profits and other benefits of ownership between upcoming family members who will work in the business and those who will not can be a ticklish task. The senior owner's desire to be fair in making that division can reverberate for a long time if the wrong decisions are made about distributing assets and income. Wise choices, though, help to minimize the dollar-driven tensions that sometimes emerge among family members and disrupt the succession process.

Many business consultants and business-owning families say that the simplest and most equitable division is along the lines of the family's business versus nonbusiness assets. The company is handed over lock, stock, and barrel to the family members who come into the business to stay. The authority and benefits of ownership thus go along with the responsibilities of management: you run it successfully, you get it. The senior generation's nonbusiness assets—real estate, securities, most of the personal property—are divided among only those family members who don't work in the business. It's a neat, clean scheme.

One of the problems with this approach, however, is that the family members who take over the business may start realizing benefits from it almost immediately, while those who are in line to get the house and the blue chips may not collect for several more years. Sister Sue, for example, becomes CEO of the family business and drives her new BMW into the company parking lot while Brother Bill nurses along his old Dodge and waits (maybe with growing impatience) for the angels to call daddy home. Even Sue may not like the arrangement if she has to give up all rights to family heirlooms or if she bridles at earning her inheritance by the sweat of her brow while Bill gets his share just for outliving their parents.

It's possible to include other family members in the ownership of the business as long as (1) they don't have management control and (2) additional incentives and rewards are provided for those family members who put their time and talent into running the company.

One useful way of doing so is a stock distribution plan that allows the family members in the business to retain voting—and therefore management—control and a reasonable share of the dividends while those family stockholders outside the business hold either a minority voting position or no voting position at all. For the sake of ownership continuity and management stability, some form of buy-sell stock agreement should be drawn up to prevent future tinkering with such a plan.

Another proven method is to put total ownership of the company in a perpetual trust with a very tight charter. The trust distributes profits as dividends according to a set schedule; the trust can be dissolved if the company is liquidated or sold, but individuals' shares can never be traded. One profitable midwestern chain of community newspapers has been owned and operated by five generations of the same family for nearly 140 years, with only negligible family disputes about the business. The family members attribute this remarkable record to the farsightedness of the second-generation owner, a clever woman who went to her richly deserved reward after ensuring that a family trust would be the sole owner of the company and that the company's general manager would always be a nonfamily member.

Taking Care of the Senior Owner

Incredible as it seems, some founders or senior owners of family businesses get so caught up in taking care of the business and the upcoming generation that they fail to take proper care of themselves. Making fair financial provisions for the retiring owner and spouse is necessary to keep the transition businesslike and to protect the long-term interests of both the company and the family.

The typical senior owner wants three results from handing over the family business to family members: confidence that the business will continue to be run successfully; a feeling that his or her experience and ideas for the business are still valued, even if they can only be given as suggestions, not orders; and a financially comfortable retirement.

A good corporate tax or financial planning expert should be brought in to help structure the senior owner's retirement plan. One group of experts at the accounting firm of Price Waterhouse suggests as possibilities a qualified or nonqualified retirement plan, a private annuity, or some other form of stock transfer such as a recapitalization of the company. The qualified retirement plan may be funded from the business's pretax profits, with the money going directly from the company to the retiring owner. The IRS tends to look at qualified plans with intense interest, since the business pays no corporate income tax on those dollars. A nonqualified plan allows the company to invest its retirement fund contributions in a variety of instruments. Those contributions may or may not be tax deductible, and the IRS watches them closely, too.

The private annuity is another option. Here stock in the business is transferred to the incoming owners in exchange for a guaranteed lifetime income for the retiring senior owner and—if the stock is held in common—the owner's spouse. Payments received are taxed like any installment sale, with that portion of each payment that represents a return on the senior owner's original investment being tax-free. A special advantage of the private annuity is that when he or she dies, the senior owner's or survivor's estate has no taxable business assets.

If something other than a private annuity is selected, the family should also agree on how the remaining business assets will be transferred when the senior owner dies. There are a number of common approaches, including Section 302 and Section 303 stock redemptions, cross-purchase agreements, insurance policies on the senior owner's life, lifetime gifts, and others. Of course, there's always the personal will that just leaves the stock and other assets to the heirs. But that approach can create estate tax problems that have forced some families to sell their businesses just to pay Uncle Sam's claim on Uncle Joe's largess. Legal and accounting specialists should be retained to put together the transfer mechanism that's best suited to the individual business and family situation.

All incentive, compensation, and retirement plan alternatives should be evaluated against what the business can reasonably afford now and—assuming that any approach worth calling a plan has an inflation escalator built in—what it will be able to afford in ten or 20 years.

Taking Care of Nonfamily Employees

Solid, evenhanded management of the transition process can go a long way in minimizing the stress on nonfamily employees of the business. Unquestionably, they will suffer some stress, perhaps caused by uncertainties about the new generation of owners, the future of the company, job security, or just the natural impact of change. Such concerns aren't necessarily specific to family business succession; they could as easily emerge if the company were being sold to an outside buyer or undergoing a major internal reorganization. But some key people might find the changing of the family guard to be a good time to start looking around. If it's possible to retain them through incentives and reassurance, it's important to do so, if only to reduce the destabilizing effect of personnel turnover.

Table 5.2 Fair Financial Incentives and Provisions

Beneficiaries	Options	Benefits	Possible Drawbacks
1. Family inside the business	Discretionary salary + profit share based on performance	Simple and fair; ties compensation to individual performance and company welfare	Requires tough-minded senior owner; family employees may object to earning profit shares
	Profits divided equally	No squabbling over unequal shares	No incentive to perform or build the business
	Uniformly high salaries + fat benefits/perks	No compensation complaints from family employees	Unreasonable financial pressure on company; no incentive to perform or build the business
2. Family outside the business	No business ownership but all other family assets	Simplest possible division method	Family inside business get no heirlooms, have to earn their share; family outside has to wait to inherit
	Nonvoting or minority voting shares in business	Family inside the business retains management control	Requires buy-sell stock agreement to control future stock sales
	Total ownership in perpetual trust	Profits distributed according to firm plan; family ownership guaranteed	Family members can never liquidate or sell stock among themselves

3. Senior owner and spouse	Company-funded retirement plan	Income for retired owner, tax breaks for business	Intense IRS scrutiny possibility for disallowances
	Private annuity in exchange for transferred stock	Guaranteed lifetime income for retired owner and spouse; no estate tax on business assets	Portion of each payment to owner taxable
	Section 302/303 redemption, cross-purchase, lifetime gift, etc.	Varies according to specific plan and structure	Varies according to specific plan and structure
	Continue lifetime ownership and transfer through owner's/spouse's personal will(s)	Owner/spouse receive profits throughout their lives	Heavy estate taxes when owner/spouse dies; no guided transition of ownership
4. Nonfamily employees	Job advancement: promotions, other financial incentives	Works well for employees motivated primarily by cash compensation	May be perceived as bribe, or create spiraling demands for advancement; salary/benefits costs
	Job enrichment: nonfinancial incentives	Less additional cost; better long-term retention	Works poorly for employees motivated primarily by cash compensation

At the same time, handing out promotions or bonuses at this point isn't always a good idea, either. Some employees and family members might interpret that as compensation for a wavering of company leadership or as a bribe to stick it out through the tough years ahead. It might be better to plan nonfinancial incentives for those jittery key people that the company can't afford to lose.

Two proven incentives for employee productivity and loyalty are job advancement and job enrichment. Job advancement, of course, is a promotion to a more responsible and better paying position in the company. Even with the extra salary and benefits costs, it is a reasonable incentive when there is a higher opening and the employee is qualified. Promotion is not so reasonable when its only purpose is to quell employee grumbling or to nail wandering feet to the floor.

Job enrichment, on the other hand, can be used effectively as a reward for good performance or, in this case, as an incentive to stay with the family business. Enrichment can include expanding a key employee's responsibilities and daily contacts laterally, assigning a new project to lead, or delegating a larger, more satisfying arena of work without increasing the employee's work load. It can mean new and more exciting challenges, more flexible hours, more comfortable working space, and better access to technical resources or clerical support. Sometimes the most meaningful job enrichment approach involves helping the employee to identify longer-term professional growth possibilities within the company and implementing a plan to pursue those possibilities. Top management's commitment to enrich an employee's job as a part of the family ownership transition process often provides more incentive for productivity and loyalty than does advancement—and without a promotion's increased costs in salary and benefits and in organizational reshuffling.

Making Rules and Setting Conditions

Robert Frost once said that writing free verse, which does not have regular rhythms and rhymes, is like playing tennis with the net down. Frost was referring to the satisfaction of poetic discipline, of abiding by the traditional rules of authorship. In managing a family business succession plan, however, there's often a lot more at stake than ending a line of verse with an exact rhyme for "orange." Making and enforcing rules and setting up conditions and criteria for handing over and taking over the family business is the most businesslike way to ensure a transfer of ownership and management authority that doesn't disrupt the business or fragment the family.

Rules, procedures, and conditions to govern the transition have to be developed by each individual business-owning family according to its specific family and business circumstances. But there are one or two general principles that should be kept in mind when the rule-making session gets down to cases.

Rules Are Necessary

The first principle is that transition rules and conditions—thoughtfully developed, circulated to all concerned, and enforced—really are necessary. Everyone—senior owners of the business, the next generation CEO and other key company officers and managers, other family members coming into the business, and those with interests but no job roles—needs to have a common understanding of how and why the succession process works. Behavioral research has shown time and again that people function in a freer and more focused manner when they know the system and its rules, the range of possibilities, and the outer limits of their choices and actions. Succession disputes and disappointments are much less likely to arise when the whole family is clear on what steps each member should take for the succession plan to succeed.

Exercising the discipline to make and enforce transition rules can be tough. But then all discipline is tough, on both the disciplinor and the disciplinee. In that respect, "You have to finish college to qualify for a management job in this company" is something like "You have to mow the lawn before you can use the car."

Setting fair and constructive rules, procedures, and conditions takes a lot of thought, time, and patience. It's another part of the succession process where the needs of the business are a very important ingredient. Having the transition rules made—or at least agreed upon—by a well-informed family council is probably the ideal way to go about it. If the task falls to the senior owner alone, it's a tougher job but still a necessary one.

Once the rules are made and announced, they must be enforced, ideally by each person's loyalty to the family's interests, sense of fair play, or family peer pressure. But if that doesn't work, enforcement is up to the person in charge. No one really benefits in the long run if anyone wheedles and needles his or her way around the conditions set for coming into the company, the performance standards established for advancement, or the ownership distribution plans. Likewise, no one benefits if the senior generation prefers to be adored rather than respected.

Authority Goes With Responsibility

However it's implemented, the linking of management authority with management responsibility is a very important rule-making principle. As emphasized earlier, the incoming family member selected to run the company must have the legal and financial authority to do it. In almost every case, this means that the person chosen to head the company must have voting control of the stock for effective management decision making. This principle can be especially difficult to apply when the family business is the bulk of the senior owner's estate. In that case, it's helpful to take a long view of the family and the business. The senior owner's desire to divide ownership fairly among the next generation should take into account that the most valuable legacy is continuity through many future generations of a well-managed and profitable family-owned company. Dividing voting stock in two, five, or ten equal pieces can hamstring the next generation of management, fragment the company, and invite future dissolution.

Milestones and Checkpoints

Someone in almost every family remembers the days of that plaintive wail from the back seat, "How much longer before we get there?" If Grandma's house was two more towns away or just past the next Howard Johnsons, the wailing usually gave way to more constructive watching and counting. Working toward a succession goal and abiding by transition rules and conditions is a lot easier for everyone when there are rational milestones and checkpoints in place for measuring progress along the way.

The conditions, criteria, and standards set up in advance to govern an orderly transfer of authority and responsibility to a new generation of owners and managers create performance milestones and checkpoints. A sequence of key transition events is outlined, perhaps some of them prerequisites for others, and both the owner and the rest of the family can mark them off as they go by.

Ray's graduating from college and joining the company as a sales representative has been planned as a necessary step for him to ascend in the family business. When Ray shows up with his sheepskin, the succession process has passed a milestone. Earlier, Victoria decided to put in three or four years as an auditor to gain experience before coming on as the family business's assistant controller. When Vickie tosses out her last business card and sits down in the family office, that step gets checked off and everybody knows the family is that much closer to completing the hand-over of the business.

Milestones and checkpoints, set up and publicized within the family in advance, are important for a couple of reasons. First, they reassure the senior owner, the incoming family members, and the employees that constructive things are happening. As each milestone and checkpoint is passed, it ought to be noted and even celebrated as an encouraging sign that the whole family is gaining on its succession goal.

Second, milestones and checkpoints provide concrete ways to measure the performance of both the succession plan and the individuals playing key roles in its execution. They can give advance notice of success or early warning of trouble. If each checkpoint is passed smoothly, that's positive feedback that everything is on track. If critical milestones are not achieved, there is time to find out why not and to take corrective action before the whole plan goes dead in the water.

An Orderly Transfer

Not all business transactions—in fact, not all businesses—are orderly all the time. But when any aspect of any business is conducted in an uninformed, ill-planned, or indecisive fashion, that business's risk index rises by several hundred points.

Ownership succession can be one of the riskier ventures in the life of any business. Unless it's managed well, there are innumerable ways it can come unglued. Siblings can disagree over renaming the company and end up in court and in the headlines. Loving parents can bend over backward to give a promising successor a chance in the top job and the company ends up on the rocks. An overly generous stock buy-out can create a debt load that puts the business in bankruptcy and the retiring senior owner in the poorhouse.

There's no absolutely foolproof way to ensure an orderly transfer of authority and responsibility, or to prevent all of the human factors hassles that can disrupt family business succession. But cool-headed and thoroughly businesslike decision making by the senior owner during the period of transition, built on meticulous succession planning, can help keep the probable risks at acceptable levels. And it could make the difference between a family business that publicly turns itself inside out and one that survives and thrives for many generations to come.

Succession Decisions Checklist

This checklist summarizes the decisions that should be made to ensure an orderly, businesslike approach to planning and managing succession.

Decisions and Actions	*Completed*
1. Select and announce the next head of the business.	————
2. Plan financial compensation and incentives. ( ) For the next CEO ( ) For other senior executives	————
3. Select or develop plans for funding the senior owner's retirement and for transferring business ownership. ( ) Owner's retirement plan ( ) Transfer of business ownership	————
4. Plan fair provisions for family members not coming into the business. ( ) Ownership shares in the business ( ) Distribution of personal assets	————
5. Make succession rules and set conditions. ( ) For successors' entry into the business ( ) For promotion and advancement ( ) For taking greater responsibility ( ) For handing over authority ( ) For handling family disputes	————

Managing the Transition

In some families, the hand-over of business management and ownership from one generation to the next is as smooth as silk. In others it sometimes seems to be a two steps forward, one step back process. But in any case, the transition doesn't run itself. It has be skillfully and conscientiously managed from start to finish.

When younger family members start moving into positions of responsibility in the company, the transition period—which may last from less than five to more than 15 years—has begun. But there are still lots of matters that require attention if the transition is to have a happy conclusion: preparing the next generation of managers and owners, rationally delegating responsibility and authority, monitoring the transition process, enforcing the transition rules, and making corrections if the transition drifts off course.

Preparing the Next Generation

Chapter 2 discussed the importance of analyzing potential successors' needs for specific training and experience to hone their abilities and give them the skills necessary to run the family business successfully. But does that mean everybody running a business these days needs a degree in business administration? Or is working at the owner's side the best preparation for eventually doing what the owner does?

The answer to both questions is yes. Running any business today is a much more complex job than it used to be. Whether a business manufactures microprocessors or grows corn to sell at a roadside stand, its activities are more tightly regulated, more frequently inspected and audited, and more subject to outside economic and social forces than ever before. Today's managers need a broad array of skills and knowledge, and business owners need to stay informed on a broader range of topics than their predecessors ever dreamed of. What's more, the complexity of the whole business environment—technology, finance, regulation, the pace of change—in the next century is certain to increase. That all spells T-R-A-I-N-I-N-G for the generation that's rising into management and ownership of family businesses.

Family Business and the MBA

What do you get when you cross a pine seedling with a marijuana plant? A Christmas tree that turns itself on. And what do you get when you send the boss's kid to the Wharton School of Business (or another reputable, accredited business school) for an MBA? A well-educated young person with the right combination of skills and a lot of potential as a manager and executive in the family company—with the emphasis on *potential*.

The MBA—master's degree in business administration—is viewed by many major corporations as an admission ticket to the executive ladder. That's because companies like IBM, for example, believe that a solid academic education in business management, finance, marketing, operations, and related subjects gives new employees basic business skills, more or less confirms a commitment to a career in business, and equips them to start learning specifically how and why the company works.

For similar reasons, studying for an MBA can be valuable preparation for becoming an executive of a family-owned business of any size or type. The higher-level abilities developed in a good MBA program—long-range strategic planning, setting business goals and guiding a company toward their achievement, analyzing market potentials and keeping a company strongly competitive, capitalization and financial management, recruiting and managing personnel effectively, selecting technologies and technical systems—are essential to building and sustaining a profitable enterprise.

But an MBA is just a neatly framed piece of paper until all that knowledge is applied to the needs and operations of a real business organization. With the total cost of getting an MBA degree currently running between $5,000 and $40,000, business schools ought to issue a performance guarantee with every diploma. They don't. Formal education alone is no assurance that a graduate will develop the detailed understanding of a company and the sensitivity to an industry and marketplace that are required for successful business leadership. For the broad preparation of a young, incoming manager and future owner of the family business, the expense and time (usually at least two solid years) required to get an MBA degree are usually a good investment. But everyone concerned should be aware right up front that additional training, guided experience, and hard work will be necessary to translate academic knowledge into effective executive management of the family company.

American business spends approximately $30 billion annually to train its executives, technicians, supervisors, secretaries, and other employees. A considerable portion of that amount pays for nondegree training and professional development: special focus seminars, short courses, update conferences or self-instructional training. This is the kind of training that IBM, for example, relies on to convert a basically skilled person with an MBA into a specifically skilled IBM employee.

Seminars and short courses are excellent for bringing family business managers up to speed on state-of-the-art technologies, new methods of production or personnel administration, and other subjects that are specific to a job or an industry. Seminars and short courses that last from two days to two weeks are offered by business schools, community colleges, and trade or professional associations. They are also available from commercial vendors such as training firms and independent consultants. Some companies hire consultants to design and conduct customized training for them, or they have their own training staff do it.

When they're done well, these short bursts of training are very effective. They bring executives, managers, and other employees into contact with experts in their field. They provide intensive training in subjects that can be applied immediately to work responsibilities: planning, finance, public relations, information management, leadership. Because they're usually sharply focused and packed with details, seminars and short courses can have an immediate impact on how incoming family business managers and future owners see their companies and themselves and how well they perform in their jobs.

My son once asked his grandfather, "How do you find a stock broker?" My father-in-law answered, "Go into the middle of a vast open prairie, out of sight of all signs of human habitation. Wait there until a powerful thunderstorm rolls in. Then, in the middle of the storm's loudest and longest crash of thunder, whisper to yourself, 'I want a stock broker.' One will show up in less than thirty seconds."

That's also a pretty reliable way to find seminars and short courses for management training and executive development. A quick scan of the advertisements in a recent issue of *Inc.* magazine yielded a count of 25 ads for executive seminars, management short courses, leadership enrichment experiences, training centers, and training consultants. The tuition and other costs per person for these open-enrollment seminars and courses start at about $75, plus travel and meals, for something like a one-day course on how to write better business letters and memos. They can run as high as $5,000 (not including travel) for a two-week retreat at an Arizona spa where CEOs learn to deal with executive stress. On the other hand, trade and professional associations' convention programs sometimes feature excellent special-focus workshops and other training sessions for no more than the cost of convention registration.

Running a company requires a combination of art and science, intuition and skill. The new generation of management and leadership in the family business can develop its artfulness and intuition through quick wit and guidance from more experienced hands. But in an increasingly complex and technologically sophisticated business world, the necessary skills can only be developed through education and training.

Experience Outside the Family Company

Many a first-time job applicant has been crushed by the catch-22 in the interviewer's question, "And how many years of experience do you have?" The applicant can't get the job without experience and can't build up experience without a job. Of course, people who apply for work in their own family's company probably can be hired without the previous experience. But on the other hand, maybe they shouldn't be.

Lucian had two sons still in diapers when he got his realtor's license and made a down payment on his first small apartment house. By the time the boys, Tom and Wally, were in high school, Lucian had built a successful business in real estate and development. He got them summer jobs on his construction crews and later brought them into his office to sit with him as he planned and priced land projects.

Like many entrepreneurs who create success from sheer talent, energy, and ambition, Lucian pushed his sons hard to come to work for him and one day take over his business. The boys joined the company just after college graduation, and Lucian put them to work doing things his way.

Wally was happy to adopt his father's methods. But after the first couple of years, Tom was chafing under Lucian's firmly fixed ideas. Tom and Lucian began to disagree often and vehemently. Finally, Lucian said, "If you think other companies are better run than mine, just go to work for one of them." Tom took him up on it, leaving to join a shopping center developer as director of strategic planning.

While Tom moved onward and upward elsewhere in the industry, Lucian and Wally plugged away at home. The company was in a decline, having a hard time keeping pace with a changing real estate market. The approaches that had worked so well for so long were getting stale. Wally was still interested in taking over the business, but Lucian was starting to worry that by the time he retired there might not be much business to take over.

When he heard that Tom was being courted by a nationally known firm, Lucian decided to make his son a better offer. Tom accepted and came back to the family business, bringing a wealth of experience and fresh perspectives and ideas: marketing and advertising plans, precision computerized forecasting of future housing de-

mand, and innovative finance packaging for integrating real estate resales with new construction projects.

In five more years, the company had turned around. Lucian put together an ownership succession plan that made Tom the next president of his diversified development and property holding company and rewarded faithful Wally, too. ∎

Admittedly, this case has echos of the return of the prodigal son. But the point is worth making anyway. During the several years he spent outside the family company, Tom was immersed in new and different ways of working in the land development industry. Maybe he could have spent that time learning what his father's company had to teach about its finances, operations, markets, and customers. Instead, both he and the family business ultimately profited from Tom's being tutored by various bosses and making his early mistakes on their payrolls. In the end, his return to his family's company was like a transfusion of healthy new blood into a tired body.

Circumstances permitting, it's generally a good idea for younger family members to work outside for a while and then come back with a commitment for the long haul. The family business gets the substantial benefits of their experience and, as psychologist Matilde Salganicoff at the University of Pennsylvania points out, they get to prove to themselves and the world that they can make it on their own. When they come into the family business, it's by free and confident choice and not because they have no other options. In sum, the value to all concerned of that outside experience is so great that whenever possible it should be programmed into the preparation of successors and not left to chance.

The Well-Managed Apprenticeship

Something else that shouldn't be left to chance is the successors' learning of the family business once they're on board. When noble traders roamed the earth, apprenticeship was the first step toward becoming a master craftsman. Apprentices not only developed their skills at the master's elbow, but they also ran errands, hauled the heavy freight, and swept out the shop after closing. Young apprentices usually worked long, grueling hours for no more compensation than the simplest room and board and the privilege of learning. But by the end of a solid apprenticeship, there was nothing apprentices didn't know about their businesses, their tools, their customers, and their crafts.

So there are good, practical reasons why learning the company from the ground up is a time-honored tradition among sons and daughters coming into the family business. The reasons are so good, in fact, that the period of apprenticeship in the family business should be planned and managed to make it the best learning experience possible for those who will be running the place in a few years. But starting out on the loading dock, working in the stock room for a few months, doing a couple of years in sales, and then coming up to the vice president's office does not an adequate apprenticeship make. Here's what does.

Goals and Objectives As with any sound educational experience, a plan for an apprenticeship in the family business should have clear goals. The best goals acknowledge (1) the position or level for which the young family member is being prepared and (2) what he or she should *be* when the process is completed. "Robert will be knowledgeable of the company's processes for product design and production, marketing and sales, and financial management." Such a goal, based on the company's future executive management needs, identifies the areas where Robert will get his experience. It also creates a sense of continuity for the apprenticeship by focusing on the manufacture and marketing of the product. And it makes it clear that Robert isn't being primed to supervise the delivery fleet.

Each component of the apprenticeship experience should have at least one objective, stated in behavioral (what he should be able to *do* when he finishes) terms. The objective for Robert's experience in product design and production, for example, might be "Robert will be able to demonstrate the company's product design techniques and illustrate the total manufacturing process from template to quality control." Goals and objectives clarify for everybody's benefit the intentions of the apprenticeship. They also separate need-to-know from nice-to-know, and they create performance measures.

The Right Entry Level A son, a daughter, or any other family member coming into the family advertising agency after a successful decade with J. Walter Thompson shouldn't have to start out as a proofreader. Beginning at the bottom makes sense for a person with no relevant experience, but it's wasteful as well as humiliating if the person has already mastered the principles of the industry in another company. Apprentices should be brought in at the right entry level in order for the company to capitalize on their outside experience and mesh it with the company's style and operating rhythms as efficiently as possible. Some businesses have even spun off a new smaller venture for experienced incoming family executives to lead as their apprenticeship for heading the entire company.

Guidance and Supervision   In training physicians, guidance and supervision during the apprenticeship process is called precepting. It's good old bedside teaching—assigning the intern a clinical task, watching to be sure the patient is poked and prodded in the right places, and then giving the intern immediate and unmistakable feedback on what was right and wrong about the diagnostic and therapeutic actions taken. The same kind of direct guidance should be provided to apprentices in family businesses, with senior employees assigned to instruct and correct incoming family members at every step. "Just go work in the design shop for a while" isn't good enough.

Performance Evaluation   Apprenticeships and apprentices should be evaluated regularly, at least every six months. Objectives should be used as indicators of performance and satisfactory learning. An apprentice who is not measuring up may be goldbricking or not really very interested. Maybe he or she is getting poor guidance and supervision, or maybe the apprenticeship is poorly designed. Or maybe the company's processes are not systematic enough to be learned systematically, a more fundamental problem. When the evaluations are disappointing, some kind of senior level intervention is called for.

Responsibility   The president of five family-owned real estate companies in North Carolina has set a clear standard for his son entering the business: "When he comes to work, he needs to prove he's the hardest worker around." For apprenticeship in this company to be effective, to have real value for the company and the apprentice, the young family member must pull his own weight and then some at every stage of the process. Family Business 101 isn't a lecture course, it's a work-study experience, and the apprentice should be a productive employee while studying at the master's elbow.

The senior owner and the company's key employees must also take responsibility for the apprenticeship. For the employees, it's a way of ensuring that the next boss is competent and understands their jobs and problems. For the senior owner, the apprenticeship has double benefits. It's an opportunity to train the people who will be taking over the business to do the tasks that will make it run successfully, and it provides a chance to measure their abilities to do those things well.

Preparing the next generation will take time, thought, and effort. Even though it won't guarantee that the family business will become a thousand-year dynasty, it's still one of the best investments that the business and the family can make in the future.

Delegating Responsibility

Dick Levin, professor of business at the University of North Carolina and a highly respected management teacher, writer, and consultant, proclaims the first commandment of business management: Thou shalt make a strategic plan! Maybe the second commandment, and a close second at that, is Thou shalt delegate! Assigning subordinates responsibilities for various components of the operation, from making the coffee to making the product, is a basic function of a good manager. Delegating responsibility is especially important during the transition between generations of ownership of the family business. And it serves several purposes.

Building Experience and Confidence

There's no better way to master a job than by doing it. The best training demonstrates new skills and then gives the trainee hands-on practice in using them. The successful family business apprenticeship is built on that principle, too. But there comes a time, such as when a person first gets a driver's license, when the instructor has to get out from behind the wheel and give the young driver full responsibility for getting the job done.

Gus had known the moment was coming from the first day his daughter Linda said she'd like a job with his mid-size publishing company. Linda was a bright, ambitious, and sweet kid, "her old man's daughter," everyone said. She was his youngest child and the only one of his children who had shown any interest in the business.

Linda had had small jobs around the office since she was a teenager. When she got serious about joining the business after college graduation, Gus methodically planned for her specialized training, a couple of years with another publishing house, and then some apprenticeship time in his editorial, marketing and sales, and finance departments. Linda did well everywhere, but, like Gus himself, she seemed to have a special gift for marketing.

The company was in the second year of flat sales, and Gus knew that his marketing approach had run out of gas. Linda had some fresh ideas and was eager to put together a new plan. She'd trained and worked in marketing, and she'd learned the publishing business in general and the family company in particular. The other employees liked and respected her. There wasn't a single good reason not to put her in charge of marketing and sales.

But when the moment came, Gus almost choked on the words. How could he give the vital job of running a vital company operation to his own baby girl? Wasn't it just a couple of years ago that she was wearing pigtails? Did she know enough to handle all that responsibility? Could she ever do things as well as he did them? What if she failed? "Linda," he croaked, "I want you to take over marketing and sales as vice president of the company."

At that moment, Linda seemed to transform into somebody Gus hadn't really seen before. A calm, confident smile came into her eyes as she squared her shoulders. "Thanks, Dad. I accept. I'll be a good vice president, and some day I'll be the second best president this company ever had." Then—Gus couldn't believe it—she actually shook his hand like a fellow executive and turned to leave the office.

Within 18 months, the company had opened a wide new market niche through direct mail advertising. The sales force came alive, and revenues bounced back to their earlier level and then kept on climbing. Linda was a strong marketing and sales VP, and a few years later Gus had no qualms about making her president. And she still is her old man's daughter. ∎

Getting Used to Not Being in Charge

Delegating gives the rising generation practice in taking responsibility and exercising authority while more experienced people are still around to act as advisors and provide a safety net. But it serves another purpose, too, because it gives the senior owner some useful practice in giving up authority.

For a person who has spent a lifetime building and running a business, it can be very hard to let go when it's time to turn the business over to someone else. One day the senior owner is in charge of a complex, active company, and staying on top of everything really keeps the juices flowing. The next day, the retired former owner is in charge of nothing but a vegetable garden, and the only juices flowing are those squeezed out of the carrots and tomatoes. Maybe the former owner is also terrorized by uncertainty about the successors' abilities to run the business over the long haul, to keep it profitable, and to keep the retirement plan funded. Suddenly there are a lot of "what if" questions and not many comforting answers.

A certain amount of post-transition letdown is inevitable. But it's less traumatic when the senior owner has tested the successors' abilities by delegating increasing amounts of responsibility and authority over the years and watching them handle it. Delegating that's honest—not just letting the successors dance while the senior owner pulls the strings—also helps a senior owner learn to live with having less and less authority. By delegating, a senior owner learns to exchange executive power for a more subtle influence within the business, and sets a practical example for successors to follow when it becomes their turn to hand the business over to a new generation.

Keeping Everyone Else Serene

Systematically delegating responsibility and authority has a positive impact on other members of the family and on the company's employees, who can watch as the next generation of managers and owners takes incremental control of the business operations. For the employees, it confirms the continuity of the business and their jobs. For other shareholding family members, it provides evidence that the new management team is solid and that everyone's financial interests are in good hands. Keeping the confidence of employees and family members reduces one potential source of significant stress during the transition period.

Monitoring the Transition Process

Among pilots there's a saying that you don't have to be very smart to fly an airplane, but you do have to pay attention.Except for the part about not being smart, something like that can be said about managing the transition process. The senior owner does have to pay attention. Weaving the new family management and ownership into the fabric of the business requires careful monitoring, from the day the changeover begins until the day the next generation is fully in charge—and even beyond.

Monitoring involves careful watching, measuring the progress of the transition against the succession objectives, rules, and criteria. It calls for keeping an eye on change and on the effects of change, within the business and within the family. And it occasionally calls for making adjustments and corrections— sometimes radical ones. It's done more easily and effectively when there's a system in place that provides for a reliable information flow and controls.

Maintaining the Flow of Information

Maintaining a reliable information flow is the first component of a transition monitoring system. As increasingly greater responsibility for performance and authority for decision making are delegated to the incoming generation, senior owners put a little more distance between themselves and their companies' action centers. That's good, because it gives them practice in not being in the middle of the action. But until ultimate responsibility and authority are handed over to the incoming generation, senior owners must keep a finger on the pulse of the business.

They will continue to read the reports and printouts that record the company's quantities and volumes, of course. But they should also stay on top of what major decisions have been made, what decisions need to be made, and what the decision-making rationale is in each case. (Actually, that's a good supervisory practice in any organization at any time.)

Some senior owners set up weekly meetings with their top managers, including younger family members who have assumed responsible positions, and get a "major decisions" report from each manager. These meetings bring important business actions out in the sunlight and permit senior owners to review them and comment on them. At the same time, they keep senior owners from interfering with the finer points of the company's operations, providing that by agreement, the meetings are the only time they can second-guess the managers' decision-making authority. If the weekly meeting will not work for a particular business, other information channels are possible. But any information flow mechanism for transition monitoring has to be not only reliable, but also open and above board.

A System of Transition Controls

A system of controls is the other necessary component of a transition monitoring system. Outside of the relatively cut-and-dried realm of accounting and finance, many people don't like the idea of controls on the human dimension of business operations. But controls are important under any circumstances because they allow the organization to deal with complexity and change, correct and minimize mistakes, and facilitate delegation. Controls are especially useful for keeping a hand on the pace, quality, and outcomes of the transition process.

Normally, monitoring controls are based on succession objectives and transition standards. In *Management*, James Stover and Charles Wankel suggest several alternative methods for defining and implementing controls:

■ *Precontrols* lay out selected courses of action and allocate resources—money, time, personnel—in advance. A project budget is a good example. Precontrols are best applied when needs and conditions can be projected, but they should be flexible enough to provide some room to maneuver if the unexpected happens.

■ *Steering controls* essentially provide an "if . . . then" kind of guidance. Standards are predetermined. The information flow provided by weekly decision reporting sessions or by the company's management information system indicates when those standards are met, and when they are, certain things are almost automatically triggered. When son Bill's division exceeds productivity targets for the fourth successive quarter, Bill gets promoted. The key is to set up the standards and then abide by them.

■ *Yes-no controls* are little more than a system of requiring prior approval for every action. It's good for exercising rigorous control, but it concentrates authority at the top, and it's a poor choice for building successors' capabilities and confidence.

■ Finally there are *post-action controls* that kick in only after the project has been completed, the decision has been made—or the damage has been done. Presumably, post-action controls prevent the same mistakes from being made repeatedly. But few managers are satisfied to wait until the end of the game to find out how things went. No senior owner should be willing to wait until the transition process is completed to learn whether it succeeded or failed.

Like many other aspects of managing the transition, selecting and authorizing a control system is usually the job of the senior owner. For obvious reasons, precontrols or steering controls provide the smoothest management of the process. For the selected system to work to the advantage of the senior owner, the successors, and the business, everyone must know that it's in place and understand how it works.

Even so, incoming young managers and future owners of a family business can be particularly sensitive to the word "control." They're chomping at the bit to take charge of things. They're ready to cut the senior generation's strings, not weave them into a rope. They want autonomy, not control. In fact, management research emphasizes that there should be no real conflict between autonomy and control in a business organization. A system of controls that lays out boundaries, states intended outcomes, provides for predictability, and decreases the need for intense supervision gives everyone ample freedom to create, develop ideas, and make decisions within defined areas of authority. A good system of controls puts it all in writing, reduces the play of whimsy in management and monitoring, and offers a clear way for both the senior owner and the rising generation to keep current with their progress.

Once the monitoring system is in place, the numerous steps and stages in the transition can be efficiently tracked. There are inside and outside transition barometers that are helpful in predicting fair weather and foul, and there are the Big Three indicators of how the business is reacting to the transition.

Inside and Outside Barometers

Most employees will give the senior owner good reports when the incoming family members are doing well. But not many will feel comfortable coming into the boss's office and declaring, "Your kid is a screw-up!" They'd rather tell themselves that incompetence or immaturity in the next head of the company is someone else's problem, not theirs, even when they know that's not true.

It's more common for young family members to make and air derogatory assessments about one another during the transition. Sometimes resentments fly hot and heavy, fueled by old jealousies or hidden but continuing anger over succession decisions: "You made him the executive vice president instead of me, and now he's spending three times as much as he should on redecorating his office." The wise senior owner maintains enough objectivity to take such criticisms with a grain of salt and to sort them out and take corrective actions based on their merits. It's important, however, not to ignore such negative reports altogether. Even if they aren't literally true, they may be symptomatic of feelings and perceptions that will corrode the new generation's ability to run the business in years to come. Conflict between family members within the business is a transition barometer. If conflict is frequent, the transition is not going well. Some changes in procedures, plans, or even people may be necessary.

The period of management transition in the family business is a time of change. New people inevitably bring in new ideas and new ways of doing things, and they should have latitude and the senior owner's support in making certain changes. But for monitoring purposes it's smart to identify who's benefiting from those changes. If it's the company, then everyone's heart is probably in the right place. But if the benefits of change are flowing to just a few persons—those family members making the changes, for instance—then it's time to review the new ideas and methods for the sake of preserving the family's business and harmony.

Another barometer on the transition process is what can be called the rhythm of the organization. Although the term is hard to define, every successful business has its own rhythm and when a company is out of rhythm, everybody senses it—especially those who've been around awhile. Things aren't getting done as quickly or as well as usual. Everyone's behavior changes a little: they're quieter in the halls and offices or they get tense or grumpy for no reason. They start losing paperwork, making math mistakes, and muttering to themselves.

If that happens, it could be the fault of the notorious ozone level in the air conditioning. Or it could be a subtle sign that people are on edge because the management transition is not taking hold very well. A few missed beats in the company's rhythm shouldn't cause the senior owner to start seeing ghosts around every corner. But they are worth checking out and clearing up.

The viewpoint of the interested nonfamily outsider is another good barometer for forecasting smooth or choppy transition sailing. The senior owner's ears should perk up if the company's principal banker keeps asking, "So, uh . . . how are the kids doing in the business?" If longtime customers suddenly insist on talking to the boss instead of the family member who has become the new vice president for sales, maybe they're just being nostalgic. Or maybe there's another reason. On the other hand, it's worth noting if bankers and suppliers and old customers are taking to the new management like ducks to water. The inside and outside barometers are good for positive forecasts as well as negative ones.

Checking the Big Three

Finally, the senior owner should monitor the transition process where the board of directors and the investors will evaluate it: at the bottom line. The Big Three outcomes of any business endeavor—productivity, growth, and profit—can be useful overall predictors of successful succession, and they should be watched and measured carefully during the transition.

In a business organization, *productivity* sometimes gets confused with activity. While activity may be no more than the movement of people, products, and papers, productivity is the measurable yield of activity. It's relatively easy for rising family managers to increase the company's activity by shortening deadlines, jacking up the minimum weekly number of sales calls per agent, or just walking around telling everyone to get (often interpreted as "look") busy.

Productivity, however, is measured in numbers: sales, production volume, and efficiency of output in relation to cost and effort. Productivity is contracts in force and dollars in the bank. It's the heartbeat of the business. Maintaining or improving productivity requires considerably more management ability than does boosting activity, so it's a good index of how well the new generation is settling in to the business.

Growth is vital in any business, because the alternatives are stagnation or decline. Unless the family company is undertaking a program of controlled downsizing for strategic reasons, it should be growing annually at some respectable rate. The new generation's capacity to sustain or improve the business's rate of growth is a pretty reliable predictor of how it will handle the future.

Then there's *profit*, one of the fundamental reasons why any company, family, or person is in business. If there's no value in making a profit, why not go into charity work? As the rising generation takes responsibility and authority, the company's profit standard—whether it's 15 percent or 2 percent—should at least be maintained, unless there are solid reasons for a fluctuation.

If profits drop because costs jump or because the general economy goes on a wild ride, it offers a good chance to test how the new generation of managers can deal with such forces. If profits drop because some people in the company decide to overcompensate themselves, that's a red flag. Of course, if profits go up after two years under the new managers, that should be saluted, and the senior owner ought to pick up the tab for a little celebration.

The Big Three outcomes usually take longer to show up as measures of the transition's effectiveness. They may indicate either deep-seated problems or great promise of success. But productivity, growth, and profit are the pillars of the family-owned business, and their strength or weakness should always be watched in monitoring the transition process.

Playing By the Rules

Recent civilization has accomplished many wonderful things, including making up myriad rules to govern people's behavior under various conditions. Traffic laws have the practical purpose of preserving lives and property. Etiquette preserves human dignity and social decorum.

The value of both kinds of rules—and of others in between— is that they provide a certain stability to our interactions and allow us to live together in an orderly fashion. Rules and conditions have similar value in helping to structure the transition of family business management and ownership, keep its progress orderly, and protect the interests of those involved. Transition rules that aren't enforced fully and fairly, however, are worse than worthless; they can undermine family relationships and torpedo the business.

For example, a senior owner declares that if each of his two sons comes up with the book purchase price of 10 percent of the stock in the family business, he'll split the other 80 percent of the stock between them as gifts and pay the taxes. The kids have six months to put the money together, but if they don't invest, they don't get the stock. One son starts negotiating with his banker. The other son celebrates his impending business ownership by plunking down $15,000 on a $120,000 Italian automobile and obligating the rest of his personal credit for the balance. At the end of six months, one brother is ready to buy stock. The other one isn't, but he's confident that Dad won't cut him out of the family business.

What's a father to do? Of course, in this case it depends on how the interests of other family members will be affected by the outcome. It might also depend on whether the son's actions confirm a continuing pattern of bad judgment.

On principle, the son has clearly not met the condition for ownership of the business. The senior owner could extend the period for the son to buy the 10 percent of the stock; if he does, he might stiffen the condition—not as punishment for the son's foolishness but to reinforce the notion that life in business is full of causes and consequences. He could cut the son out of the business completely on the grounds that anyone who can't play by the succession rules can't be trusted to own the company.

Probably the worst thing the owner could do is to say, "Boys will be boys" and just give his son the stock. The other son could justifiably go through the roof. And even though succession is a family matter, the whole world is watching the transition process. If the rules aren't enforced thoroughly and fairly, the company's credibility in the business community may suffer.

Sometimes the toughest businessperson turns out to have insides of strawberry jelly in the face of family wheedling and needling over transition rules. A few tears, a few pleas for parental clemency, a family member's threat to walk out of the business and the family if he doesn't get his way—and the whole succession plan falls apart as the rules and conditions go out the window. When that happens, the parents seldom end up with the gratitude and undying devotion of satisfied kids. They more often end up watching the business being mismanaged while listening to their offspring grumble that it was a bum company when they got it.

In other cases, however, the businessperson who's always been a real sweetheart turns out to have insides of barbed wire at succession time. Senior owners who have a lot of their identity and self-esteem wrapped up in the business may see transition rules as eroding their power and threatening their control over their own lives. They may be tempted to bend the rules in their own favor and not stick to their side of the succession bargain. This most frequently happens when the agreed-upon time comes for the senior owner to delegate major decision-making authority or to finally step down. The incoming generation becomes frustrated and angry, and the carefully organized succession plan falls into shambles.

The advantage in knowing that transition rules might be broken—by the senior owner, the next generation, or both—is that remedies can be considered in advance. The best business strategy includes contingency plans that can be activated if strategic targets aren't met or assumptions don't prove to be valid. Every law on the public books is accompanied by a prescription for redress or punishment if the law is disobeyed. Most families take no pleasure in punishing one another for infractions or offenses. But for the sake of preserving the business, the family's succession plan should provide everybody with a fallback—possibly even a legally enforceable one—if the transition rules are broken.

When the Transition Plan Isn't Working

The poet Robert Burns once wrote, "The best laid plans of mice and men aft gang aglay." When a man named Murphy finally figured out what Burns was trying to say, he restated it as one of his laws: "If something can go wrong, it will."

Sometimes, despite everyone's best intentions and best efforts, management and ownership transition runs into trouble. Rules are broken, conditions aren't met, someone dies unexpectedly. But like the juggler with ten plates in the air, the family can't just walk away from the situation. There's too much at stake. A lot of business-owning families have made it across some terribly rocky ground during the transition period, and their experiences can teach some valuable lessons.

Fine-Tuning the Plan

There's no plan so good that it can't stand fine-tuning. Not tinkering, meddling, jiggering, or diddling—just careful fine-tuning. Sometimes a slowdown or a breakdown in the transition process requires just a little fine-tuning to get things up and running again. For example, if someone gets divorced during the transition, it may require fine-tuning the distribution of ownership. If Action A takes two years longer than anticipated, then the timing for Actions B and C may have to be adjusted.

The senior owner and the family have to be willing to maneuver in response to changing conditions. But be cautious: the maneuvers should be limited to those that are really necessary—no hitting a fly with a sledgehammer—and all fine-tuning should be done with the knowledge of everyone concerned.

The Interim Manager

Chapter 2 described an unfortunate kind of family relationship that can seriously threaten successful succession: long-standing competition, bitterness, or anger that separates parents from their children. The optimism surrounding succession planning may temporarily push a conflict into the background. But unresolved conflicts can resurface when outgoing parent-owners and incoming young family members are interacting closely during the hand-over. Even when plans are solid and all the objective criteria have been met, underlying feelings can be so intense that the senior owner literally cannot bear to hand over the business to the successor, and the successor cannot bear to accept the business from the senior owner.

In this case, the family may decide not to pursue a direct hand-over but instead to put in an interim manager to act as a buffer between the generations. A senior nonfamily employee or a qualified executive manager from outside the company is hired on a fixed-term contract. The transition plan is modified (which will require more than just a little fine-tuning) so that management control is passed from the senior owner to the interim manager, who becomes a cutout and also a sort of surrogate successor. Later, after the senior owner completes a graceful exit, the interim manager turns over control of the business to the successor. By buffering the unresolved hostility that has blocked transition, the family's succession goals for sustaining the business are ultimately met.

When the Kid Just Doesn't Cut It

Some situations are so profoundly difficult that even an interim manager isn't an adequate solution. For example, the designated new boss can't, or won't, do the job that needs to be done. His or her deficiencies in management and leadership have been pointed out. Poor performance and violations of critical policies have been documented. Training, counseling, and good advice have had no effect. A lot of time, money, and effort have been invested in trying to correct the problems, but nothing has worked. The company is in trouble, and the senior owner faces the prospect of firing a family member, possibly even a son or daughter.

Sometimes succession prospects are problematic from the very beginning. But, driven to see the business continue, the senior owner may purposely overlook the warning signs. The analysis of family members' qualifications is fudged by a senior owner who's convinced that he or she can make an effective company president out of an unmotivated or even uninterested son or daughter. Transition rules are ignored, standards are lowered, and decisions are made too hastily. To the central question "Can this business be handed over to this family," the senior owner knowingly gives the wrong answer.

Several years later, revenues are in a slide, employee morale is down, and the company is wallowing without strategic direction or leadership. It's grimly clear that the successor isn't going to cut it. The senior owner shouldn't be surprised. Deeply disappointed, perhaps, but not surprised. Maybe the successor is against the ceiling of his or her competence. Maybe the successorship is just a mismatch of one individual's abilities with the requirements of a particular job or company. What options do the senior owner and the family have for correcting the problem before it becomes a catastrophe?

There are standard ways to terminate a nonfamily executive. There are polite and straightforward ways: a ranking board member or senior owner can have a quiet chat with the executive, state the reasons for the board's dissatisfaction, and offer him or her an attractive severance package. Or the executive can be called in, given a royal reaming, and ordered to be out of the building in thirty minutes. There are also insidious ways: the board can send the message by cutting the executive's compensation to ribbons or replacing the executive on the policy executive committee with a junior clerk, approaches that have all the class of a rattlesnake in the mailbox.

These standard methods can be—and sometimes are—used to remove a younger family member from company leadership. Biting the emotional bullet and going ahead with an outright, up-front termination may actually be the cleanest solution and a favor to everyone, yet some families will not find it acceptable.

If a successor has gotten used to a job and its perks and has no prospects outside the family company, he or she is unlikely to see the light and leave voluntarily. Perhaps the successor has been persuaded by past encouragement that, by golly, he or she is a pretty good executive after all. Being told at some late date that it's time to go because the company is in a shambles would be quite a shock, and the reverberations of the erstwhile successor's anger and suspicion could hit the company and the family like an earthquake.

Each family that faces this crisis has to handle it in its own way. There are no stock formulas. But here are three approaches that can often accomplish the inevitable with minimal damage to all concerned.

Dilution of Authority   The board or senior owner can reduce the authority of the young family executive, and therefore any negative impact on the business, by redefining the executive's job. Executive-level development and review of operating policies and procedures can be assigned to a committee. Approval authority can be decentralized to unit managers. Top management decision making can be put under the control of a front office management team. The board or one of its committees may become the de facto chief executive of the business. Maybe the company's traditional, buck-stops-here executive management style will have to be abandoned, but that's better than having the company self-destruct.

Reorganization   Similar to dilution of authority, but more radical, is breaking out the operating divisions most vulnerable to top-level ineptitude into subsidiaries or other self-contained revenue centers. These new units are managed by divisional presidents or directors who are given authority that for all practical purposes equals that of the nonfunctioning company president. They report to the board through the company president, who becomes essentially a well-compensated figurehead.

A variation on reorganization involves spinning off a new venture from the parent company and putting the ineffective CEO in charge of it. Perhaps a smaller and more focused operation will be more compatible with the executive's ability and style. The CEO gets to be in charge of something and so saves face while the larger business is saved from poor leadership. As with any other form of gambling, the company probably shouldn't invest more money in this approach than it can afford to lose.

Sale of the Company   Some families have chosen to sell or merge their closely held businesses rather than to put the skids under unsuitable family executives. With the help of financial planners and lawyers, they have either found a single buyer or taken the company public and then cashed out their stock. Everyone ends up with a wad of money but no company, and the family executives end up with no jobs. Sometimes the cold, hard prospect of having to sell the company is enough to stiffen the senior owner's resolve to handle a management problem more directly.

Except when unforeseeable events (at the level of death or destruction) crop up, severe succession problems need not happen at all. When they do, it is usually the result of inadequate succession planning, lack of thoroughness in analyzing business needs and family qualifications, or inattentive transition management. Managing the transition is demanding because it's the detailed process of implementing the succession plan, making sure it works, and making sure it sticks. At the same time, the transition period is rewarding for the senior owner and for the family because it creates the confidence that the business will continue into the next generation as a family business.

The Transition Management Checklist

This checklist is designed to help keep tabs on the major things that require management, monitoring, or general attention during the transition period.

Action Item	Planned	Underway	Completed
Preparing the Next Generation			
Confirm gaps between business's needs and current/prospective successors' abilities	____	____	____
Arrange formal business education (MBA) for key incoming family managers	____	____	____
Arrange special-focus seminars/short courses for rising family executives	____	____	____
Plan/arrange for family members' experience in industry outside of family company	____	____	____
Plan/manage/evaluate apprenticeship within family company	____	____	____
Delegating Responsibility			
Identify management slots/responsibilities to be delegated to young family employees	____	____	____
Plan for increasing responsibility, decision-making authority of rising family managers	____	____	____
Monitor effects of delegation on young managers and results for business	____	____	____

Monitor effects of   ____   ____   ____
delegation on employees,
senior owner, other
family members

Monitoring the Transition

Set up transition   ____   ____   ____
monitoring system and
implement transition
controls:
    ( ) Precontrols
    ( ) Steering controls
    ( ) Yes-no controls
    ( ) Post-controls

Monitor changes in the   ____   ____   ____
Big Three:
    ( ) Productivity
    ( ) Growth
    ( ) Profits

Playing By the Rules

Monitor family members'   ____   ____   ____
and senior owner's
attention to rules and
conditions

Impose penalties for   ____   ____   ____
breaking succession rules

Revising the Plan When It Isn't Working

Fine-tune the plan   ____   ____   ____

Hire interim manager   ____   ____   ____

Terminate or dilute   ____   ____   ____
incompetent management

Letting Go: When, How, and How Much

There was a time when ownership and management authority was transferred from one generation to the next with much more dispatch than finesse. History tells story after story of the crown prince who grew tired of waiting for his aging royal father to hand over the throne. Finally, with a shout of "Let's get on with it, f'cryin' out loud!" the prince had the old boy dragged out and beheaded. The new generation took charge, and the family kingdom stayed in the family. Of course, the transition was a bit abrupt. But when, how, and how much to let go was less of an issue.

Some senior owners of family businesses can't wait to turn it all loose and get on to other things: "The day the kid walks in the door, I walk out, and that's it—I'm off to Florida!" For many others, however, the hardest step in the whole succession process is finally letting go—cleaning out the desk, hanging up the title, taking a last look around the office. In either case, letting go cleanly, graciously, and in just the right measure is the key to everything that follows.

Why Letting Go Is Important

There are three reasons why it's important to let go when the appointed time comes. First, by that point in the transition process the next generation of family owners and managers should be at the peak of readiness to take over. Second, most businesses can't tolerate two generations trying to sit in the boss's chair at the same time. Finally, the contract between the senior owner and the successors must be honored.

In the 1920s, Carl's father left the farm and used his inheritance to buy a small local insurance company. He'd gone on to build a three-state empire in banking, insurance, and newspaper publishing. Carl joined the business and became expert in running and expanding the family companies, and just before his father's death he'd taken over as majority owner and protector of the family's business interests. He immediately started to plan for passing the business to his sons, daughters, nieces, and nephews. The transition went smoothly, and his overall succession plan arrived at the point where Carl was to retire and make the final hand-over of authority.

But when Carl looked retirement in the face, he balked. "Not just yet," he repeatedly told the family. "Another few months, maybe, but not just yet." The successors were at the peak of their executive powers, they had considerable management responsibility, and their expectations were high. Like trained race horses held too long in the starting gate, they were getting very restless. But at age 76, Carl was still in full control of his faculties and the majority of stock in the business.

As years passed, the situation deteriorated. The newspapers went into a slump. When the family's banks got stuck with a lot of bad real estate loans, Carl stubbornly refused to let the younger managers make adjustments in capital reserves, and the feds came down like a swarm of locusts. "He's running the business into the ground!" family members told one another and anyone else who would listen. Morale drooped, and family mem-

bers and employees began to snipe at one another. Carl's oldest son, the president of the family's central holding company and the chairman-designate, ran out of patience and accepted a lucrative job offer from a California insurance company.

Six months later, Carl suffered a stroke that, as even he realized, left him unable to continue to run the companies. He stepped down, and his son-in-law became chairman and chief executive officer. By that time, though, both the family and the business faced a long, difficult rebuilding process. ∎

Carl was a strong and capable executive and an enlightened senior family business owner. Through foresight and careful planning for succession, he had brought the business and the next family generation to an optimal point for hand-over. But when the time was right, he couldn't put the final touch to a lifetime of management and leadership success by handing over, turning loose, letting go. The consequences were disruptive, though thankfully not disastrous, but if Carl had been willing to follow his own succession plan, there would have been no unfortunate consequences at all.

Who's In Charge Here, Anyway?

No company, regardless of how large or diverse it is, can tolerate multiple bosses for very long. When the younger generation takes over and the senior generation continues to try to call the shots, open warfare is almost inevitable. The business starts to look like the crowd at a tennis match, with heads swiveling between the contestants as everybody tries to figure out who's winning, who's losing, and whose court the ball is in now.

The focal point of final authority for management decision making must be clear, even if that point is the majority vote of an executive team or a board of directors. Having two individuals or factions trying to run a family business at the same time clouds that focus, to say the least. If the senior owner continues to give orders and exert influence while the new CEO is trying to install a new management mechanism, the business is likely to come unglued, with some employees and family members remaining loyal to the former management and others following the new leadership.

Without cohesion, the company's quality and quantity of output declines and interested outsiders—bankers, investors, customers—start to lose confidence. Or the business may just go on hold, waiting for the leadership issue to be settled. When and if the dust clears in the executive suite, it usually takes quite a while to rebuild the company's momentum. The bottom line is that a family business cannot tolerate extended control disputes and remain a business for very long.

Honoring the Contract

A succession plan is a contract among members of the family (1) when buy-sell agreements, private annuities, or other components of the plan are executed as legal documents or (2) when the senior owner proposes a plan for the continuity of the business and the rest of the family agrees to it, with good faith on both sides.

The first kind of succession contract has a clean, hard edge to it, and the underlying power of the law is there to give it real muscle. In many ways, a legally binding succession agreement is the most rational way to go. One reason is that family and business relationships may become scrambled—through death, disability, divorce, or other unforeseen events—and a binding contract will help to maintain order in the succession. Of course, a good lawyer can often get even the best contract invalidated in court, and there's a chance that some family members are waiting for a shot at doing just that.

By contrast, implied contracts, developed and agreed to by the family in good faith, have all the legal muscle of a jellyfish. Their only potential for enforcement is their moral and ethical potency, and so they become tests of how the values of the family act on the values of its business arrangements when the chips are down. If the senior owner reneges on a good faith agreement to step down either on a specified date or when the incoming generation has met specified conditions, it's unlikely that the successors can get a judge to enforce it. But it's not too naïve to believe that there are strong forces at work nevertheless, because it is morally imperative that the senior owner live up to the lifetime of trust that the family has invested in him or her and honor the commitment.

In any case, the senior owner must let go of control when the appointed time comes for the same reasons that one aerial acrobat must let go at the precise instant that the other one grabs hold. It's an essential part of the total plan, the partners are ready and expectant, and failure to do so can bring the whole act—and everyone in it—crashing down.

Coming Down Easy

Letting go is a planned, rational act that often drags a lot of irrational baggage along behind it. But sometimes it's easier for the senior owner, and potentially more beneficial for the business, if letting go involves changing a relationship to the company instead of dropping out altogether. Just because the business changes family management and ownership, it shouldn't toss aside the outgoing senior owner's wealth of experience, capability, and hard-won wisdom. Unless family dynamics or the atmosphere of the transition would rule them out, there are several important contributing roles that the old guard can play in the new hierarchy after letting go of control.

The CEO Emeritus

The least active new role is CEO emeritus. The title "emeritus" is attached to the retired senior owner's last position ("Chairman Emeritus," or "President Emeritus"). It's a totally honorary title, conveying recognition and respect but no power or privilege, although some companies provide an office, some secretarial help, and other courtesies to a chief executive officer emeritus.

If the retired owner is listed as CEO emeritus on the letterhead, the company can benefit from name continuity, which the outside world often counts as reassuring evidence of corporate stability. The new generation gets this benefit free of salary costs and without having to share management authority.

Having an emeritus title also gives the retired senior owner a sense of continued rank in the company. In the larger scheme of things, it's probably something of a throwaway. But most former heads of businesses would agree that as a designation of status, emeritus beats unemployed.

The Senior Statesman

Someone who has spent a lifetime building and running a family-owned business has developed a pool of personal and professional contacts that can be of continuing value to the company. At retirement, he or she is a candidate for senior statesman.

A family business's senior statesman may also have an emeritus title with little or no salary or be a paid consultant. This person's role is to represent (but not to commit) the company to special clients, the industry, government regulatory agencies, or the world at large. The senior statesman is free from the hassles of daily management and responsible to no one but the new CEO and perhaps the board. He or she can use a personal address book and the weight of experience to open doors, convey messages, root out business information, test the waters, lay negotiating groundwork, and conduct targeted public relations efforts—none of which might have been practical when he or she was still identified as the corporate CEO. The retired owner can enjoy the genuine importance of the senior statesman's role and a sense of continued productivity, while the new management gets the benefits of having a person who is known in and knowledgeable of the industry carrying the company banner.

A caveat: For this role to work without the senior owner either feeling burdened or feeling licensed to exercise false authority, there should be a written description of the range and the limits of the senior statesman's role.

The Part-Time Consultant

A great number of both family and nonfamily businesses include a period of postretirement consulting in their senior executive contracts. A paid consulting relationship provides income in addition to retirement benefits, and it makes the retiree's business or technical expertise available to the company on an as-needed basis.

In planning to stay on as consultants, however, senior owners should remember their own experience of employing consultants when they were the boss. By definition, consultants are paid only to consult, give advice and make recommendations, undertake problem-specific analyses, and write focused reports. Consultants are not paid for (and usually are barred from) running loose around the company, poking into whatever interests them. In most circumstances, a consultant's specialized expertise is only one tool in corporate management's kit. A consultant's advice may be taken or rejected, and the choice rests with the company.

On the other hand, retired owners serving as consultants can be important assets to companies without having to shoulder the entire burden of them. They can concentrate on what really interests them and not worry about a thousand other operational details. For example, a retired senior owner who was trained as an engineer but had to set technical interests aside to run the company might truly appreciate a chance to work only on engineering problems again. As a consultant, he or she would also have the satisfaction of starting a job, finishing it well, and then walking away. That kind of absolute closure on a piece of work can be a blessed change for someone who has lived and breathed a business for thirty or more years without a break.

The Teacher

Teaching the apprentices what they need to know to run the business is one of the senior owner's vital transition functions. In some family businesses, that honorable teaching role continues in a more limited way after the transition is completed. The retired owner's teaching can focus on transferring additional management skills, but it can also work to transfer the business's corporate memory.

Even when a company has a good system for recording and retrieving information, the mind of the man or woman who put the business together or who led it for many years is often the most dynamic source of corporate history. The company's old files can tell the new management what the family business did and when and how. But all the inside reasons why the company took certain actions are often hard for younger managers to understand 20 years after the fact unless there's someone knowledgeable around to teach them. A few shortsighted new owners and managers may be uninterested in how and why things used to be done, but most will understand the value of a corporate memory.

Of course, the retired owner's role as teacher goes beyond merely recalling the gossip and murky details surrounding corporate decisions in a bygone era. In helping their successors to interpret specific events or the chain of actions and reactions that brought the company to its present condition, retired owners as teachers-in-residence give them invaluable insight that would otherwise cost many years and many mistakes to acquire on their own.

The Analyst and Planner

The functions of analyzing a company's total business environment and outlining long-term plans for managing growth are often given low priority by executives embroiled in running daily operations, especially in smaller- to medium-sized businesses. Yet analysis and planning of the company's future become more vital as the business environment becomes more complex, the competition becomes sharper, and business economics become more volatile. Leading the company's analysis and planning functions can be a critical new role for the retired family business owner.

These functions are important because they allow a business to anticipate, plan for, and manage the inevitable long-term changes in its marketplace. A company that does not systematically gather business information and analyze it for impending changes risks being blindsided by new technologies, legislation, economic fluctuations, or the competition's strategies. If it doesn't systematically plan to deal with those changes, the company resembles poor Pauline, tied to the tracks as the locomotive of the future comes roaring down on her.

Many retired chief executives are particularly well suited for the analyst/planner role. They have years of experience in the company and the industry. They may have already done a specialized analysis of the business and drawn up a strategic plan for ownership and management succession. If they also have the confidence of the new executive management and are willing to learn strategic analysis and planning methodologies, they're ready to go to work.

Serving as the family business's chief analyst and planner can become a 150 percent–time job. The senior owner may work harder after retirement than before. Consulting help is available to set up an analysis and planning system that conforms to the company's current market position, resources, and long-term goals. After that, the retired owner becomes the corporate analysis and planning guru, reporting findings and making strategic recommendations to top management and fulfilling an important function in the family business.

Creating a new role for the retired senior owner will work only if (a) the new role is actually important to the company and not a put-up job, (b) the retired owner is actually qualified to fill it, and (c) the retired owner's continued active presence

TABLE 7.1 New Roles for the Old Guard

Role	Positives for		Negatives for	
	Retiring Owner	New Owner	Retiring Owner	New Owner
CEO Emeritus	Nice title No burdens Some amenities Continued presence	Name continuity No interference No salary costs	No authority	Continued presence
Senior Statesman	Continued activity Use contacts/skills No operational responsibilities	Valuable contacts Name continuity No authority Little/no salary	No authority Little/no salary	Continued presence May need to be controlled
Consultant	Continued activity Income Focused work	Access to skills Familiar with company No authority	No authority Can recommend but not decide	Continued presence May need to be controlled
Teacher	Continued activity Valued role No operational responsibilities	Good continuity resource	No authority	Continued presence
Analyst/Planner	Continued activity Critical role Focused work	Critical role Familiar with industry/company	Can be burden Can recommend but not decide	May lobby for old agendas

in the business is viewed by all concerned as positive and constructive. If those conditions are met, summarized in Table 7.1, both the retired owner and the new generation of management can benefit immensely by keeping the old guard on board.

Maintaining the Monitoring

Chapter 6 emphasized techniques for monitoring the transition process. But the need for the senior owner to stay in touch with the family business doesn't end when the transition is completed and management authority has been transferred. As long as the retired owner has any stake in the business, he or she should maintain an appropriate level of monitoring and be ready to provide input when it is requested by the new management. Here's why.

> *Pete had stood a long and successful watch as head of his family's business, a chain of drugstores in Arizona. He and his brothers had taken over the company from their father nearly 25 years before and had overseen its growth and increasing profitability. As the oldest son and the majority stockholder, Pete had carried most of the management load. So when the three brothers agreed that the time was right for them to step down and let the next generation take over, Pete was the happiest one in the bunch. He'd always wanted to retire to the California wine country, and now he was eager to hand over his responsibilities and be on his way. Just send the checks to Sonoma.*
>
> *For the next few years, Pete and his wife spent many satisfying evenings sitting on their front porch and looking out over the rolling hills and vineyards. He remained on the board of directors, but he rarely attended meetings and didn't even read the reports too closely. The retail drug business was the last thing on Pete's mind until one sunny morning's mail brought a letter from his son, the company president. It announced that the business was in such serious financial trouble that it was necessary*

to reduce dividends and make some adjustments in expenses, including payments to Pete's qualified retirement plan.

As Pete caught the next plane to Phoenix, he had a sinking feeling that he was already too late. In a week of meetings and going over the records, Pete learned that his son and two daughters had begun feuding with his brothers' kids almost as soon as the parents left the state. So much time had been devoted to family squabbling and maneuvering that nobody was minding the stores. A discount drug chain had moved in with a lot of buying power and slick advertising and had gobbled up a huge chunk of the family company's market overnight.

"How could you let this happen!" Pete demanded. "Where were you when we needed you!" his kids demanded in return. But when all the shouting was over, the handwriting was still on the wall. Pete could either sit in Sonoma and watch the company go down like the California sun, or he could come back from retirement and work to save it. ∎

Pete helped rescue the family business by putting in emergency downsizing and management reorganization. As he went through the process, he saw painful evidence of all the danger signs he'd missed because he'd turned off his monitoring system the day he turned over the company. Pete's case is a good illustration of why letting go shouldn't mean losing touch.

Good Ways and Bad Ways to Stay in Touch

Along with reading the routine reports, the best way to keep up with the family business is to stay in touch with the people who are running it: asking the right questions in a supportive manner, offering to help evaluate proposed new strategies, and generally showing a nonthreatening interest. Naturally, a retired owner has to remember that he or she is no longer running the company. While a retired owner may deserve more access to business information than does the stranger on the street, the new management should not be crowded too closely.

Another good way to stay in touch is by maintaining contact with the company's environment, marketplace, and key outsiders. Reading the trade press and having occasional sociable chats with the business's bankers, suppliers, and customers can help a retired owner to keep current with general and specific conditions affecting the company. Of course, playing a new role within the company instead of dropping out entirely puts the retired owner in a better position to stay informed.

Unfortunately, staying informed can sometimes look like nosing around, getting in the way, or trying to undermine the new management's authority—especially if that's exactly what the retired senior owner is doing. There are innumerable bad ways of maintaining the monitoring of the business after the hand-over. One of the worst ways is downright spying—reading mail on people's desks, going through the confidential files, or pressuring employees for information and gossip.

It's also bad form to end-run the new management by pushing the company's bankers and customers for details on financial transactions or asking any outsider directly for an opinion on how the successors are running the business. Friends and sympathetic persons will feel uncomfortable with the question, and the unsympathetic may see it as a golden opportunity to fan the flames of family dissent.

The retired owner has both a right and a responsibility to continue to monitor a business that has been transferred to younger family members. The right belongs to anyone who is financially invested in the company and counting on a reasonable and reliable return. The responsibility is more specialized. It belongs to the person who's invested his or her life in the family business and believes in it as a family heritage that's worth preserving.

Giving and Accepting Advice

Monitoring the business after the hand-over means being ready, willing, and able to contribute to the company's ongoing success, support its solid new initiatives, or give appropriate assistance if things start to get a little confused. Giving and accepting advice on running the business can be a tricky transaction for a retired owner and the new family management. Sometimes it just can't be done without suspicion and conflict. Even in the best situations, giving and accepting advice constructively takes a lot of openness, mutual respect, and self-confidence on both sides. These guidelines based on the experience of business-owning families may help.

Don't give advice unless and until it's requested.   It's hard to keep a tightly buttoned lip when someone else seems to be bringing the business to ruin—especially if that someone is the same kid that flunked tenth-grade math, wrecked the family car, and never cleaned up his room. But the kid is no longer really a kid, he's the head of the company. Until he perceives the need for input, an experienced perspective, or the wisdom of his elders, he's probably going to brush it off as one more gratuitous dressing down from the old man. If advice is going to have constructive impact, it's got to be funneled into an open and receptive ear. It's got to be asked for.

Advice can be asked for in a lot of different ways, of course, and "Please tell me what I should do" is the least common way between kids and parents. Something like "This situation is causing us some real problems" is more common, and "I'm thinking about (cancelling the account) (buying a new machine) (firing the SOB)" may be the most common of all. The retired owner has to keep an open ear, too, and be ready to respond clearly but supportively, however the call for advice comes.

Ask for advice when the situation calls for it.   On the other side of the equation, the younger family business owner and manager should not hesitate to request or act on the senior generation's advice. After all, those older people are the ones who got the company off the ground, or kept it rolling, or built it into the successful enterprise it is today. Advice can be taken or it can be left alone, but when someone else's insight would be a help, the business's senior owner is a good person to start with.

Don't say "You're doing it all wrong!"   That's like taking out a splinter with a chain saw. Everyone's attention is focused and the job gets done, but the approach causes a lot of unnecessary damage, and the next time help is needed, it's going to be sought from another source. Giving good advice on solving a business problem requires a lot of information: How did this start? Who's involved? What's the fallout potential? Nobody likes to give information under duress. Also, most people tend to turn their receivers down or off at the first hint of belligerence or accusation. It's unlikely that even the best advice is going to be accepted if it's offered on the cutting edge of a saber.

The best advice is based on experience, not opinion.   Advice put in terms of "I think you should do it this way" sounds like an opinion. Suggestions of strategies or solutions are more credible when their past success in the family company or in other similar situations can be cited. Giving advice, in fact, is a great opportunity for the retired owner to practice his role as teacher. Even so, a younger CEO of the family business may decide to adapt the senior generation's approaches to problems, not to adopt them whole cloth. That's okay, too.

Remember the difference between giving advice and giving orders.   People don't ask for orders but they have to take them; they ask for advice but they don't have to take it. An order says "I want you to," while advice says "Maybe you should"; that's a critical difference to the person in the center. The retired family business owner may no longer be in a position to run the company by giving orders, but he's in an invaluable position to influence its future by giving advice.

How Much Control to Retain—and How

Responsibility for running the business must be accompanied by authority to make executive decisions. This first commandment of family business succession has been preached from page one of this book and from every consultant's pulpit in the land. It's also generally assumed that real authority gets its strength from control—of vital information, finances, and voting stock.

So if the continuity of the family business is achieved by giving it to the kids, that means giving them full responsibility, full authority, *and* full control, right? Well, . . . almost. In fact, it's a good idea for the business's senior generation to retain some degree of control even after the hand-over is done. It's a way of promoting the preservation of the business, continued growth and profitability, the fair distribution of proceeds, and adherence to family values. It checks and balances the actions of a new, eager management and supplements without weakening the oversight of the board of directors. The critical questions are what kind of control, how much control, and how to retain it.

What Kind of Control and How Much?

Control doesn't refer to ironfisted tyranny or the means to jerk people around at will. The proper kind and degree of control for a retired owner to retain ensures the new management's accountability, not servitude. This control is exercised through maintaining enough leverage to be sure that management accounts for the business's financial status and activity, consults before taking the company in radically different strategic directions, and justifies adoption of new policies that affect the retired owner's interests.

How to Retain Control

Control can be retained either by hanging onto the prerogatives of ownership or by invoking the influence of the family. As an example of the first, some senior owners hold back just enough stock to qualify as a significant voting power. Keeping ten or 15 percent of the business doesn't give them a majority, so there's no annulment of the marriage of management responsibility with decision-making authority. But they are satisfied that it guarantees a hearing for their views in the boardroom— or if not there, then (in most states) in the courtroom. The stock is held personally or in trusts administered by trustees who are committed to the senior owners' interests and prepared to steadfastly protect them.

An alternative way to maintain postretirement control is to orchestrate the influence of the family to keep management of the business on an even keel. A new family CEO who has been screened by a thoughtful planning analysis and prepared through a carefully managed transition period is unlikely to turn into a maverick after taking charge of the company. But stranger things have happened when people have finally found themselves in long-sought seats of power.

Freewheeling or inept management by the younger generation can usually be controlled within the family by using negotiation, arbitration, or family gunboat diplomacy. For these control tactics to work, family members must understand that their financial or nonfinancial interests in the business are affected by the new management's behavior. That means that the family must know what its interests are in the business and how management behavior affects them. This may take an educational effort, because some members of business-owning families don't know much more about their businesses than the return address on the dividend checks.

A Negotiated Solution   Roger Fisher and William Ury of Harvard University define negotiation as the process of reaching an agreement that helps all interested parties to achieve a mutually desirable goal. Good negotiation, perhaps carried out between the retired owner and the younger CEO, is a particularly effective way to control family business management because it doesn't require anyone to lose in order for someone else to win. In *Getting to Yes*, Fisher and Ury advocate a style of negotiation that focuses on a problem, which can be separated from individuals' emotions, instead of focusing on personalities or positions, which can't be.

In negotiating to bring management behavior back into line with family interests, the problem should be stated objectively; for example, a two-year decline in profits and dividends. It should not be stated as the new CEO's bullheaded insistence on buying every new production technology that comes off the designer's sketch pad. Negotiation then becomes a process of reviewing the merits and drawbacks of alternative solutions to the problem instead of attacking and defending opposing positions.

When practiced in good faith, negotiation works as a steering control on the family business. It focuses management's attention while minimizing the exchange of unsupported opinions, name-calling, and "I told you so's" in settling business differences. It also works as a precontrol if the new CEO is convinced that the retired owner will rush back to the negotiating table if the company appears to be drifting off course.

Going to Arbitration   Arbitration is a somewhat bigger fist, but it's still wrapped in the velvet glove of rational discussion among disagreeing family members. Unlike negotiation, someone loses something in an arbitrated settlement. As used in business as an alternative to litigation, arbitration is most effective when the parties have agreed in advance that they will bring in an arbitrator—an informed but totally disinterested person—in the event of a dispute and that they will be bound by the arbitrator's findings. A few very cautious business-owning families have written binding arbitration clauses into their succession plans.

Arbitration can be applied to controlling family business management when negotiation hasn't worked or when the concerns of the retired owner and the rest of the family are at the boiling point. Under those conditions it's probably impossible to find a family member or friend with absolutely no prior attachments to either side and no interest in the outcome. An outsider acceptable to all concerned is identified as arbitrator. He or she can be an attorney or a management consultant for smaller businesses and smaller problems or, in the case of a large company with a whopping dispute, someone secured through the American Arbitration Association or another arbitration agency.

Under the rules of court-authorized arbitration, the arbitrator is both judge and jury. He or she runs the proceedings, hears evidence (including hearsay), examines the merits of both sides' positions, reviews relevant laws and documents, and issues a ruling. The arbitrator's ruling is then validated by the court. The ruling is final and cannot be appealed except on the narrow grounds of conflict of interest or gross procedural error.

Arbitration can be more informally applied to a family business dispute. A qualified third party can arbitrate the disagreement according to accepted procedural standards and issue findings and recommendations that favor either one side or the other, or perhaps split the difference in some constructive way. If everyone concerned abides by the arbitrator's decision, the immediate problem is resolved and management control is reinforced.

If someone cheats on implementing the arbitrator's recommendations and there are big bucks or big principles at stake, the rest of the family often goes to court. This course of action may or may not satisfy the offended persons. It is guaranteed, however, to produce eternal enmity among family members, lots of local headlines, raging speculation about the stability and future of the business, and a herd of lawyers that suddenly need to do income averaging. The savage succession fights of the Bingham family, former publishers of the *Courier-Journal* and the *Louisville Times*, and frequent and abusive court battles of the department store Belk family of Charlotte, North Carolina, provide stark illustrations. If at all possible, litigation should be avoided as a way to resolve disputes or to apply controls to management in a family business. Even if negotiation and arbitration haven't worked, there's still one more possibility.

Family Gunboat Diplomacy   Family gunboat diplomacy is to the family business arena what international gunboat diplomacy is to global politics. They both work by making a quick, strong, and very persuasive show of force when talking has failed. The intent of family gunboat diplomacy is to corral and control the leadership of the family business by marshalling the total influence of the family and playing a short game of hardball. Here's how it can be applied.

Less than three years after Vic retired as CEO and turned the family's successful wine importing business over to his son James, things started to get out of control. James had worked hard and productively for the company for several years, and he'd developed some ideas for expansion and diversification. Most of them seemed pretty good to Vic, so he'd written them into the company's five-year strategic plan. James took over and announced the dawn of a new age.

Sure enough, the company's international activity picked right up. During his first two years as CEO, James himself spent almost ten months in Europe to develop new agreements with grower cooperatives and shippers. His expenses were high, but James explained "Gotta spend money to make money." Not many new labels were entering the inventory, but James telexed from Paris "Takes more time to make deals over here." Without the head man in the home office, domestic marketing and business operations in general started to go slack. James responded, "Hey, I pay the vice presidents to handle the small stuff."

Because of the family's increasing concern, Vic had several talks with James about the company's major problems. They negotiated management changes required to reach the company's strategic goals, but then nothing changed at all. The family commissioned a well-known business consultant to arbitrate the growing disagreement. James initially accepted the arbitrator's recommendations, then put out a memo withdrawing his acceptance. At that point, Vic was ready to see the board throw James out, even if he had to go back in himself.

The family decided to rescue James instead of demolishing him. But they showed him just how bad things could get if he didn't turn around. Through their networks of contacts, family members squeezed both the company's and James's credit lines. They challenged every management motion before the board; James had to fight for approval of even the smallest item. The clincher was the country club executive committee's discussion of whether to continue James's membership. The family worked quietly, but they made sure James knew where his troubles were coming from.

James soon announced new plans to adopt most of the family's recommended management changes. He asked the board to approve hiring a mid-level director of corporate development to travel the European circuit, and he got busy recultivating his U.S. markets and running the company. He voluntarily reduced his own expense account ceiling "as a demonstration of management's vigorous efforts to control operating costs and improve profits." Within a year, Vic and the rest of the family agreed that the company was back on track and that James was behaving like a responsible CEO. ■

Family gunboat diplomacy is effective in direct proportion to the family's willingness and ability to apply powerful and well-organized across-the-board pressure on the maverick CEO. Not all families have the financial, political, or social clout to make family gunboat diplomacy work. Some families reject it as being too mean or unseemly. And sometimes it fails because the younger generation of family management turns out to be totally impervious, invincibly arrogant, or blind.

But as a last-ditch effort to control errant management and keep a family business dispute within the family where it belongs, family gunboat diplomacy is better than most other alternatives. It can create hurt feelings and even bitterness among family members, but it seldom creates the rank hatred and fragmentation within the family and the business that grow out of hurling charges in open court.

The Last Hurrah

For the senior owner who is stepping down from leadership of the family business, finally letting go involves a lot more than just handing over the keys to the CEO's office. It culminates a complex and often tiring process of transition. Letting go is a statement that the longest and most important part of the senior owner's life, the years spent building and running his business, is winding down.

For some senior owners, letting go is an expression of both satisfaction with their lifetime work and faith in their successors and in the future. For others, it feels like giving up and accepting banishment. For most, though, letting go is probably a little bit of both. Planning and managing the succession of family business ownership can be one of the most demanding things a businessperson ever does. But that last step, letting go when the business's continuity into the next generation has been secured, can be the most satisfying moment since nailing that first earned dollar to the wall. It's a rite of passage, the time for a celebration, not a wake, and it ought to be big, loud, and happy.

_____

The Letting Go Checklist

This checklist will serve as a reminder of the knots to be untied and the strings to keep intact when it's time for the senior owner to let go of the family business.

Ready	*Set*	*Let Go*
Is the next generation fully ready to take over?		Yes _____ No _____
	Is the retiring senior owner set for a new role in the business?	Yes _____ No _____
	Are mechanisms set to continue monitoring the business?	Yes _____ No _____
Will new management be ready to ask and receive advice if it's needed?		Yes _____ No _____
	Are appropriate controls set, and is everyone aware of them and their purposes?	Yes _____ No _____
	Is the "last hurrah" celebration planned?	Yes _____ No _____

Summing Up

This chapter reviews the planning and management activities that are required for family business succession to have a fighting chance. Figure 8.1 summarizes those activities, with references to the chapters where they are described in detail. In summing up the steps, stages, and processes, this chapter emphasizes the three characteristics of successful succession: planning, preservation, and optimism.

Planning, Planning, and Planning

Most businesses founded by individual entrepreneurs or growing out of family enterprises do not continue beyond their founders' working lifetimes. They fold, they get sold, or they otherwise cease to exist as business entities owned and operated by the founding families. Of the businesses that continue into the second and third generations of family ownership, a few are blessed

FIGURE 8.1 Review of Planning and
             Management Activities

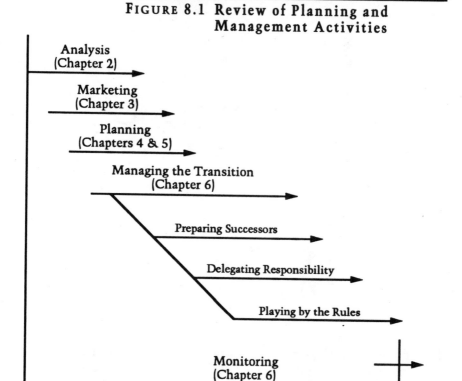

with incredibly good luck. Most, however, survive for three simple reasons: planning, planning, and planning.

Starting on Time

Succession planning should start early, probably as soon as the
business gets past the fight-for-survival stage and achieves real
momentum. When the founder decides that the business is solid,
profitable, personally rewarding, and worth hanging onto, planning for succession should begin. A second- or third-generation
senior owner of a family business should start even earlier.

The Analysis Phase

The first step in succession planning is to thoroughly analyze the business's status and needs, the family's qualifications for future ownership and management, and the senior owner's management style and expectations for a successor generation. Analysis can be difficult in lots of ways, even tedious. But it's important because of the subtle truths it reveals about the business and the family, and because it produces valuable information to be drawn upon in later succession planning steps and during the period of management and ownership transition.

Making a Market

Succession planning calls for marketing the business to the family and vice versa. Marketing educates the family in general and potential successors in particular about the business: what it actually does; how, where, and why it works; and what principles, technologies, and individuals make it function successfully. Marketing should give potential successors a realistic but largely favorable view of each aspect of the family business, (assuming the senior owner has a favorable view), but emphasizing the view from the CEO's chair of the company and how it works. The senior owner's perspective is the most useful marketing tool of all, and the dinner table review for prospective successors, their spouses, and other key family members is the most effective marketing medium.

Making the Succession Plan

As the family becomes more knowledgeable about the business and develops a genuine interest in coming in and perhaps taking over, a serious succession plan should be laid out. The best succession plans are put together jointly by senior owners and key members of their families, but the process should be directed by the owner. Because the owner has the longest perspective and the greatest stake in the plan's ultimate success, he or she is the natural person to be in charge.

A complete succession plan structures the business's next generation of ownership and management. It lays out rules and conditions for successors, and it sets up a schedule for the handover of responsibility and authority. It names names, and it announces early in the game the senior owner's choices of the next chief executive and other managers. The plan makes financial provisions for both generations during and following the succession transition: compensation, stock transfer, retirement funding. It's objective, realistic, and businesslike, and it's based on a strategic view of the company's long-term goals and needs.

The well-turned family business succession plan is not a pair of cold stone tablets handed down from the mountain. But whether or not it's a legal document, it is a contract between individuals and generations of the family. It's a detailed framework for business decisions and family interactions over a period that will probably extend well beyond the current owner's lifetime. A succession plan is essential to the continuity of the business under the founding family's ownership.

Managing the Transition

Managing the hand-over process, the period of transition between senior and incoming generations, requires a firm hand, a clear eye, and—because nothing ever works perfectly—a flexible approach. During the transition period, the senior owner must see to it that the next generation is prepared for the duties of management and ownership. Compensation, retirement, and ownership transfer plans are put into action. Managing the transition includes (1) delegating increasing responsibility to successors for decision making, (2) enforcing the rules and conditions of succession, and (3) monitoring progress and making adjustments. Usually a good plan will require only minor adjustments, but in some cases they may involve replanning the succession, reorganizing the company, or even firing the new head of the business.

Letting Go

When the transition is complete and the new generation of owners and managers is fully prepared and in place, it's time for the senior owner to complete the hand-over and step down. This is the point of the whole succession plan, the final milestone. A graceful letting go by the senior owner, who then accepts retirement or new challenges but maintains enough active influence to support the younger generation while ensuring its full accountability, is the capstone of successful succession.

Planning cannot be overemphasized. It is the key to succession. Every step in the succession process should be guided by a plan, and every transition event should be evaluated against that plan. Handing over a family business without a plan is virtually impossible.

Keeping It All Together

Planning and managing the continuity of the family business is a lengthy and sometimes difficult process. Putting everyone through it makes no sense if at the end the family is as happy as a bunch of kids on Christmas morning but the business is in tatters like so much ripped up wrapping paper. On the other hand, shoe-horning younger family members into ownership of a marginal or unsatisfying business virtually guarantees that they won't hold onto it.

Preserve the Business

Lea's Laws for Preserving the Family Business are simple and straightforward. They apply to every succession situation, every size of business, and every type of family. They are based on the premise that handing over the family business is an empty gesture if there's no business left to hand over.

Law #1: Don't play Santa Claus with stock, assets, or management authority. Succession planning is not an organ donor program where the vital parts of the business get passed out among the children and grandchildren in hopes that someone can make good use of them. For the body of the family business to survive, it must remain in one piece under competent care. If the heirs insist that something valuable has to be parceled out, make it the cuff link collection.

Law #2: Organize succession to meet the needs of the business, not the successors. If the business survives now, it's more likely that the successors' needs will be met in the future.

Law #3: Make transition rules and enforce them. Rules and conditions are essential for a systematic and orderly transfer of authority and responsibility. The person in charge should be firm and businesslike even if it hurts, because the alternative can be chaos in the family and disintegration of the business.

Law #4: Pay attention to the transition process.   There are lots of transition stages and steps to manage and monitor. The transition period can be tricky because it's both a business process and a family activity. It must be kept going and kept on track.

Law #5: Let go, but stay in touch.   When the transition is finished, the senior owner should be neither a backseat driver nor a phantom passenger. The younger generation may need experienced help every now and then. The business may need it, too.

Keep the Family in Business

Cajoling or coercing potential successors into joining the family business is unpleasant, unfair, and risky. Rather than take the time and effort necessary to market the business to the family, some senior owners try to force the continuity of family ownership by making threats, instilling guilt or putting undue pressure on their sons and daughters or other family members. If family members do not have a genuine commitment to the business, coercion won't keep the the family in business for very long.

Long-standing tensions over who's in control within the family can get carried over into succession planning, with the senior owner using the financial rewards of business ownership to bludgeon successors into submission. This approach violates Lea's Law #2 for preserving the business, and it doesn't do much for the family, either. The kids usually seize the first opportunity to reverse the power flow—the senior owner's incapacitation, for example, or a shift in board membership—and discharge their pent-up frustration on the business, one another, and their predecessor's plans and wishes. Successful succession demands that family bickering and unhealthy emotional conflict be kept in check.

Keeping the family in business also requires honesty. The new generation of family management shouldn't walk into any hidden traps or unpleasant surprises. Debts, personnel problems, and other encumbrances on the company's operation should be objectively detailed. It's neither honest nor fair to hand successors a beaten-up business while representing it as being in prime condition. They'll resent the deception, and they'll resent being made to look incompetent if the company later collapses under the weight of problems they didn't create.

Ownership and management succession is a business transaction and a family experience that happen simultaneously. Some senior owners take the position that family is family, and business is business, but that doesn't work for all families. In fact, most successful succession situations—especially when founders are handing over to the second ownership generation— work because of a meshing of gears between the business system and the family system. Successful succession meets the needs of the business for solid leadership and of the family for financial security and personal satisfaction. There's usually a little grinding and clanking as the two systems come together, but ultimately both the family and the business move forward together.

Some Causes for Optimism

Words and phrases like "hard work," "frustration," "tricky," and "disintegration" have been used a lot in this discussion of family business succession. Every one of them honestly applies to the less appealing possibilities of the succession process. But such words as "satisfaction," "rewarding" and "celebration" are equally true and honest descriptors of the process.

Increasing the Chances of Success

With a thorough analysis and a carefully prepared plan, the chances of successful succession are probably better than 75–25 going in, and there are ways to improve them still further. The first is to have *confidence in a positive outcome*. This isn't blind faith, or a naïve disregard for what can go wrong. It's a conviction that the family can mobilize itself, make a plan, put the plan into motion, work through any problems, and come out okay. Rational confidence coupled with a dedication to working hard to reach the goal is infectious. It can go through a business-owning family like Montezuma's revenge through a bus full of tourists, although with a more positive effect.

Another way to increase the chances of succession success is to *believe in the next generation's capacities* to master the art and science of business management and ownership. Some succession efforts never quite succeed because the senior generation never quite accepts the next generation as its equal. It's psychological blindness to hang onto outdated images of runny noses and teenage awkwardness when people have already proven themselves to be competent, responsible adults. "The body achieves what the mind believes" is a YMCA motto for encouraging young athletes. Similarly, a successor's ability to achieve is helped immensely by the senior owner's willingness to believe when it comes to their assuming responsibility for the family business.

Finally, it helps to remember that *a parent and a child are entirely different people*—even though they may share many genetic and cultural traits, laugh at the same jokes, or wear the same size shoes. Phrases like "chip off the old block" and "spittin' image of the old man" tend to blur this fact and its importance to successful succession. Parents and children often have different priorities and see the world, their families and the family business from different perspectives. Even if they make similar or compatible business decisions or career choices, they may make them for different reasons. So owners do not simply pass the family business from the right hand to the left. The business is passing from one individual to another individual. Ignoring successors' distinctiveness as individuals may make accepting them as owners and managers unnecessarily difficult.

Cheery Thoughts for Those Darker Moments

Families that have successfully owned and operated businesses for two or more generations have some encouraging words for those who are just starting to think about succession and continuity. Some of their stories and comments can be downright inspirational when the succession process starts wearing everyone down. Here are a few of the gems, with the sources' names changed to protect the guilty as well as the innocent.

The Best Gift in the World

Jim and Betty Jean, of Sparkle-Tone Carpet Cleaning: *At first, we never thought of our business as anything* *except a way for us to earn a living. We started out with a little franchise that did pretty well, so we decided to sell the franchise and move out of state and start a similar business from scratch. The business started doing better and then all of a sudden it was doing a lot better. We were only in our late thirties and taking home over $100,000 a year, and we said, "This is something worth passing on to the kids if they want it."*

Well, teenagers don't see carpet cleaning as very glamorous, but we put them to work weekends and summers on the trucks and in the office anyway. And later they began to realize that meeting people and providing a good service was satisfying. And they saw they could have a pretty good income, too, if they worked hard enough and used a few smart techniques and common sense in managing the business.

As it turned out, our daughter married and moved back east, so our son and daughter-in-law are the ones who really want to take over the business when we retire. They've finished their educations and learned just about all we can teach them about the business, so we'll step out of their way in another five years. It's going to feel good seeing them running a business that we built with our hard work. We've set up the transfer so they'll buy us out at a good price over quite a few years, but in a way it'll be like giving our kid the best gift in the world. ∎

The Second Time Around

Peter, of Crossman and Sons, Architects and Engineers: *My father started the firm in the 1940s and did very well in postwar housing construction. My brother and I finished our architectural training in the mid-70s, and Dad suddenly made quite a thing over wanting us to come right into business with him. We loved our father, but we didn't want to be the boss's sons, so we went our own ways. That really hurt Dad's feelings, I guess, and the three of us went through some stormy years before all was forgiven.*

One Thanksgiving, Dad surprised us both by showing us a plan he'd put together for my brother and me to come back to his company, move into senior partner positions when we proved we were ready, and then become full owners when he got ready to retire. We spent the whole weekend talking about what his firm was doing and how its future looked. We went over Dad's plan and made a few changes, but we could tell he'd really thought everything out very carefully. He'd even hired a consultant to sketch out compensation proposals that were close to what my brother and I could earn at firms in bigger markets.

Over the next six months, the three of us spent a lot of time together. Dad never pushed us, as he'd done before. He just treated us like fellow professionals that he was trying to recruit into his firm, and we looked him and the business over as we would anyone who'd offered us jobs. There was some negotiating, a little wrangling, but in the end we came up with a solid package. Also, we all just felt very good about working together and keeping the family name going in the industry. Dad retired last year, but my brother and I have agreed that the firm will always be called Crossman and Sons.

A New Twist in a Long Line

Bert, of Olympic Industries, Inc.: Our family has been in the tool manufacturing business for more than 100 years. We've restructured a couple of times and diversified into related industries—came damned close to losing it all in the 30s—but family ownership has been continuous through four generations, and the company is stronger now than it's ever been. A lot of that success has been due to the fact that the family has not only owned the company and maintained good conservative policies, but it's always been able to produce sons and daughters to run it, too.

Ten years ago, though, I found myself as president and chairman of this $200 million corporation, majority owned by about 25 family members, with no idea how this business could stay under family management. My own kids just didn't seem to have the interest and the ability it would take to step into my place when I stepped out of it, and neither did anybody else in their generation of the family. It was like looking around a football stadium where there are plenty of expectant, cheering people up in the bleachers but nobody coming out on the playing field. I sure didn't want to be re-

membered as the CEO who gave up family management of the company.

One of our outside directors, a man my father and I had asked to stay on past the usual retirement age because he was such a help, came up with an idea. "If you can't grow new family leadership naturally," he told me, "you'll have to build it from the ground up." So I got together a team of family stockholders and senior employees to do an analysis of the company's history and long-term strategy, and from their report I drew up a list of leadership abilities and characteristics that the company would have to have at and near the top over the next 20 or 30 years.

Then we got some consultant help in putting together an in-house orientation and training program for family executives and a couple of other senior nonfamily people we really wanted to keep. It was focused exclusively on our industry, our marketplace, and our company's senior management needs. It was designed to immerse people in the company while teaching them how to run it. The program ran for three years, and halfway through, by God, two people in the program were pulling away from the pack as strong contenders for my job. One of them was my own son.

I've announced my plans to retire at the end of next year, and the board has announced a successor to run the family company. He's my own kid, and he's going to be a great CEO, if I do say so. Keeping this business under family ownership and management for another generation required a special—for our company, even radical—maneuver. But it was worth it. ∎

Last-Minute Crisis

Maureen, of Slotkin's Jewelers: *I've never seen my husband Ted as crushed as he was that night when he came home from the store. "They want me out," he said. "They want me to retire and get out right now." When Ted was very young, he bought his uncle's jewelry store. It was in pretty poor shape, but Ted thought he could make something out of it. So he gave up the idea of going to college and put his whole heart and soul into building up that business. Sometimes I can still taste all the peanut butter sandwiches we ate during those early years.*

*Well, he made it, and when the boys were grow-
ing up Ted was always telling them what a great opportunity
they had ahead of them because he'd teach them everything
about the retail jewelry business and one day they would have
the store. Ted had planned every detail, and it all worked out.
The boys finished college and came to work with him. Several
years later Ted and I made our retirement plans—get a smaller
house, travel a lot, winters in Florida.*

*But Ted had put so much of himself into the
business that when the time came he just couldn't leave it.
"The boys aren't ready," he'd say, or "I'm not sure they can
afford to hire my replacement yet." Finally, I guess, the boys
got so frustrated—and I can't really blame them—that they just
told him it was time for him to retire. It hurt Ted and made
him angry, and it scared him a little, too. He didn't want to
feel unneeded by his children, and he didn't know what he'd
do with himself when he retired. It was the one thing he hadn't
planned for. Our family had been through some hard times
together, but we'd never had a crisis like that.*

*The boys came over to the house together. They
were sorry they'd been so blunt, they said. They thought there
was a way to make everybody happy. They suggested that Ted
turn over management to them and become chief buyer for
the store. He'd make four trips a year, and he'd keep up with
his old friends among the jewelry makers and wholesalers. Ted
agreed right away that it was the perfect job for him, because
all along his ability to buy well was one of the main reasons
for the success of Slotkin's Jewelers. The crisis was over, and
although it hasn't been a total retirement, it's been a great
retirement ever since.* ∎

You Just Never Know

*Lu-Ann, of Dress Designs: I wish I'd started plan-
ning much earlier for my daughter and son-in-law to take over
my business. I spent every day, year in and year out, looking
only at the inventory and the books and the advertising. I
didn't see much beyond next season's new lines and the next
customer coming through the door. I was able to open three
new stores, though, and the business did real well—right up
to the day I got sick. I'm so thankful the kids were willing to*

jump in and help, but they really didn't know anything about the business, and it almost went down the drain. People in business who have kids that might be interested in coming into the business and hanging onto it should make plans, plans, plans. Maybe those plans won't work out. But you just never know. ∎

An Eye on the Future

John, of Midstate Printing and Engraving: *If I could talk to every family that owns a business and wants to keep it in the family and pass it along to the kids, I'd tell them one important thing: Keep your eye on the future. The family isn't just one person or just that person and his kids. The family will go on into the future. Think years ahead. Make your plans so that the business will be in the family when your great-grandchildren get old enough to take it over. Now that's a family business.* ∎

The Power of the Family Business

Every society has institutions that shape it, give it cultural sub-stance, reflect its history, and foretell its future. Religion, the forms and subjects of artistic expression, and the economic base are among them. Because it's an essential component of our society's economic and social structure, the family-owned and -managed business is such an institution.

Of course, that elevated notion doesn't help much when profits are plummeting, the employees are all down with the flu, and the kids are fighting over who's going to inherit the best parking place in the company lot. But it's worth bearing in mind, because when building, running, or passing along the family business gets rough, it helps to take a long view of the importance of the enterprise.

There is power in the family business and in the family that owns a business. This power exceeds social position or wealth because it comes from being vital to the growth, stability, and character of society. Family businesses exercise that power when they produce more efficiently than most other business organizations, when they demonstrate clearer values and a higher ethical standard than many other businesses, when they show the strength of their roots in the communities that nourish them by returning large measures of goodwill and philanthropy, and when they sustain continuity of ownership and management. Being a member of a family business, growing it, handing over or taking over its leadership, and plotting the steady course of its future are powerful actions. Any way you look at it, family business is a good business to be in.

If this book has done its job, said what it should have said and been worth its price, the business owners and family members who have read it should now have a little better understanding of the human complexities of succession in the family business. They should also know what other families have done and what they can do themselves to survive and prosper. Finally, they ought to have a sense of optimism that with planning, hard work and maybe some luck, they can make everything work out alright.

Selected
Bibliography

Chapter 1

Some of the basic statistics on life expectancy, place in the national economy, and longevity family businesses' are from "Managing Continuity in the Family-Owned Business," by Backhard, R., and W.G. Dyer, Jr., and Davis, P., "Realizing the Potential of the Family Business," *Organizational Dynamics* Summer 1983; and Dingle, D.T., "Passing Down the Family Business," *Black Enterprise* June 1984.

The list of characteristics of family businesses that survive succession is from Ambrose, D.M. "Transfer of the Family-Owned Business," *Journal of Small Business Management* January 1983.

The observation about many family businesses' relations with lending institutions was made by Dailey, R.G., et al., "The Family Owned Business: Capital Funding," *American Journal of Small Business* July 1979.

Smith Bagley's role in the RJR/Nabisco leveraged buy-out is recounted by Burrough, B., and J. Helyar, *Barbarians at the*

Gate: The Fall of RJR/Nabisco. New York: Harper & Row, 1990.

Chapter 2

Davis, cited above, also stimulated thinking on the three types of families and how they fare in business.

The national survey that uncovered senior business owners' concern for being fair to their children in succession planning appeared in Emshwiller, J.R., "Handing Down the Business," *The Wall Street Journal*, May 19, 1989.

Peters, T.J., and R. Waterman, *In Search of Excellence: Lessons from America's Best Run Companies.* New York: Harper & Row, 1982.

Chapter 3

The tendency of family businesses to be run as big, happy families has often been noted. See "A.P.A. Makes the Short Haul Profitable," *Business Week*, October 6, 1973.

Leon A. Danco has pointed out that family businesses also have a capacity for complacency and stagnation. See "Family Companies: A Mixed Bag", *Industry Week*, March 1, 1971.

Chapter 4

The need for transition rules and conditions has been cited by Ward, J.L., and L. Sorenson, *Keeping the Family Business Healthy.* San Francisco: Jossey-Bass, 1987.

Emshwiller, cited above, also refers to beginning succession planning 15 years before the owner's retirement date. The author who suggested starting when the heir apparent is eight years old chose to remain anonymous.

Consultant Neal Wehr's view that money is the chief cause of succession conflict is quoted in Hamilton, P.W., "The Special Problems of Family Business," *D&B Reports* July/August 1986.

Chapter 5

Joseph Mancuso points out the importance of taking care of details in *How to Start, Finance and Manage Your Own Small Business.* Englewood Cliffs, N.J.: Prentice-Hall, 1984.

The concept of the "lucky sperm" was reported by Emshwiller, cited above.

Maslow, A., *Motivation and Personality*. 2nd ed. New York: Harper & Row, 1970.

More information on minimizing taxes in family business stock transfers can be found in the Tax Information Planning Series, published by Price Waterhouse.

Chapter 6

Advertisements for seminars, courses, videos, and various other training devices were counted in *Inc.*, October 1990.

Dr. Matilde Salganicoff was quoted in Nelton, S., "Shaky About Joining the Family Firm?" *Nation's Business*, (November 1983).

Todd Cohen described the five-company North Carolina corporation. "Triangle Families In Business," The News and Observer, Raleigh, N.C., October 1, 1989.

Dick Levin says "Thou shalt plan strategically!" and a great deal more that's useful in *The Executive's Illustrated Primer of Long-Range Planning*. Englewood Cliffs, N.J.: Prentice-Hall, 1981.

The ideas on controls in transition management owe a lot to Stoner, J.A., and C. Wankel, *Management*. 3rd ed. Englewood Cliffs, N.J.: Prentice-Hall, 1986.

Srully Blotnick outlined the role of the nonfamily buffer manager in "A Gift to Your Children," *Forbes*, July 30, 1984.

Chapter 7

Fisher, R., and W. Ury, *Getting to Yes*. New York: Penguin Books, 1981.

Suggested Readings

Succession

Alcorn, P.B. *Success and Survival in the Family-Owned Business*. New York: McGraw-Hill, 1982.

Bork, D. *Family Business, Risky Business*. Chicago: AMACOM, 1986.

Danco, L.A. *Beyond Survival: A Business Owner's Guide for Success.* Reston, Va.: Reston Publishing Co., 1975.

Danco, L.A. *Inside Family Business.* Cleveland, Ohio: Center for Family Business, Univ. Press, 1985.

Rosenblatt, P.C. *The Family In Business.* San Francisco: Jossey-Bass, 1985.

Sources of Assistance

The following organizations have strong national reputations as sources of information and consulting assistance for family business in general and for succession planning in particular. However, the author makes no representations as to the ability of any of the following to assist successfully in a particular family business situation.

National Family Business Coucil
8600 West Bryn Mawr Avenue
Chicago, IL 60631

Wharton Family Business Network
The Wharton School of Business
University of Pennsylvania
3508 Market Street
Philadelphia, PA 19104

Institute for Family Business
Baylor University
Box 8011
Waco, TX 76798

Center for Family Business
5862 Mayfield Road
Cleveland, OH 44124

Center for Private Enterprise
Loyola University
820 North Michigan Avenue
Chicago, IL 60611

The Family Firm Network
2169 Union Street
San Francisco, CA 94123

Index

A

Accountants:
  in pre-planning analysis, 23
  in succession planning, 94–95
Advice, 170–172
Advisor groups:
  employees for succession planning, 98–99
  family for transition rule-making, 127–128
Ambrose, David, 8, 9, 195
American Arbitration Association, 175
Analysis, pre-planning:
  of the business, 22–28, 182
  of the family, 28–37, 38, 114–115, 182–183
  of the owner, 37, 39–47, 183
Analyst and planner, retired owner as, 166
Apprenticeship, 138–141, 157
Arbitration, 174–176
Assets, dividing, 72–73, 120–122, 123, 128
Attitude of the senior owner:
  as factor in business survival, 9
  in marketing, 54–56, 60, 76, 183
  in succession planning, 40–45
  in transition, 151
Attorneys:
  as arbitrators, 175
  in succession planning, 93
Authority:
  decision-making, 109
  dilution of, 155
  equal to management responsibility, 128
  giving up, 143
  transfer of, 161

B

Bagley, Smith, 15
Benchley, Robert, 28
Boss, selecting the next, 112–118, 183
Business associates in succession planning, 97–98

C

Career choices, successors', 2, 22, 54–55, 61–62, 64, 79, 138
Character of the business, 24–28
Checkpoints, transition, 128–129
Compensation, 118, 119–120, 154
Competition, 63–65
Consultants:
  in succession planning, 92–93
  management and family business, 95–97
  retired owner as, 164–165
Continuity (*Also see* Succession):
  checking its importance, 21–22
  into 3rd generation, 13–15
  successors' attitudes toward, 54–55, 62–63, 64–65
Contract, succession, 160, 162, 184
Control, retaining, 11, 40–41, 172–177
Controls, transition, 145–147
Costs of succession:
  to the owner, 66–69
  to the successors, 65–66
Courier-Journal and *Louisville Times*, 175

D

Davis, Peter, 31, 195, 196
Delegating, 141–144, 157
Directors, board of:
  role in public sale, 68
  role in succession planning, 91

E

Emeritus, CEO, 163
Employees:
  as transition barometers, 147
  in the apprenticeship, 141
  incentives for, 126
  in succession planning, 98–99
  reassuring and retaining, 78–79, 123–124, 143–144
  view of the business, 25
Entrepreneurs:
  analyzing the entrepreneur-owner, 40–42

children of, 96
retaining start-up management
  style, 95
textbook example, 2
Ewing, Gloria, 120
Executive, owner as, 42–43, 47
Experience:
  of successors outside the family
    business, 136–138
  of the retiring owner, 163
  advice based on, 172

F
Family:
  assessing members' skills, 32
  coherent family, 29, 30, 31, 32
  employees, 119–120
  independent family, 29, 30, 31,
    32
  influence on the business, 7
  interdependent family, 29, 30, 32
  leadership of, 43–47
  matching with business, 2, 15,
    48–49
  outside the business, 120–122,
    143–144
  relationships affecting succession,
    11–13, 15, 64–65, 187
  system vs. business system, 6–7
  working in the business, value of,
    9, 12
Family business:
  compared with other businesses,
    6, 60, 193–194
  definitions, 5–8
  impact on economy, 6, 193
  life expectancy, 8
  managing, 6, 27–28, 62, 67, 95–
    96, 145, 173
  non-family manager, 114, 122,
    152–153, 154
  preserving, 108, 185–186
  problems, 26–27, 186–187
  productivity, 149, 193
  specialist in, 96–97
Firing a family member, 153–154,
  184
Frost, Robert, 124

G
Getting To Yes (Fisher and Ury),
  174, 197

Gunboat diplomacy, 176–177

I
Inc., 136, 197
Information:
  after the handover, 169–170
  for analysis and planning, 166
  for transition monitoring, 144–
    145
In Search of Excellence (Peters and
  Waterman), 43, 196

J
Jordan, Michael, 76

L
Leadership:
  as a compensation factor, 120
  early identification, 116
  of the family, 43–46
Levin, Dick, 141, 197
Litigation, 174, 175–176, 177
"Lucky sperm," 114, 197

M
MBA, 134–135
Management (Stover and Wankel),
  145, 197
Mancuso, Joseph, 110, 196
Marketing:
  creating a favorable image, 58–60
  choosing outlets, 69–72
  defining appeal, 60–63
  pricing, 65–69
  sizing up competition, 63–65
Monitoring:
  during transition, 144–150
  following the handover, 168–172
Motivation and Personality (Maslow), 117, 197

N
Negotiation, 174
Non-business needs and interests,
  10, 36–37
Non-family manager:
  buffer between generations, 152–
    153
  instead of unqualified family
    members, 114

running family newspaper chain, 122

O
Ownership, transferring, 72–73

P
Planning for succession:
  importance of, 9, 11, 12, 16, 83–86, 181
  objectivity in, 87
  realism in, 88
  goals, 88–89
  timing, 85–86, 90, 182
  role of the board, 91
  role of outsiders, 92–99
Price Waterhouse, 122, 197
Public stock offering, 67, 68, 73–74, 94, 155

R
Retirement:
  facing, 143, 160
  new roles following, 163–168
  planning financial provisions, 122–123, 126
RJR/Nabisco, 15, 195–196
Rules, transition:
  need for, 127–128
  checklist, 131
  enforcing, 150–152

S
Salganicoff, Matilde, 138, 197
Selling the business, 155, 156

Senior statesman, retired owner as, 163–164
Strategy:
  marketing, 53, 56, 57, 63, 72, 77, 78, 183
  in planning, 88, 109
Succession (*Also see* Continuity):
  disputes, 45, 64–65, 96, 97, 115, 121, 147, 152–153, 161-162, 174–177, 186, 187
  reasons for failure, 2, 9–11, 12–13, 37–39
  reasons for success, 2–3, 8–9, 15–16, 37, 187–188
  into 3rd generation, 13–15
  plan, structure and purpose, 99–106

T
Teacher, retired owner as, 165
Training:
  as a continuity factor, 9
  as a succession cost, 67, 106
  for the company's specific management needs, 34–35
  for modern business complexity, 134
  training sources, 135–136

W
Wall Street Journal, 32, 114